WHY ME?

Coping with Grief, Loss, and Change

PESACH KRAUSS
and Morrie Goldfischer

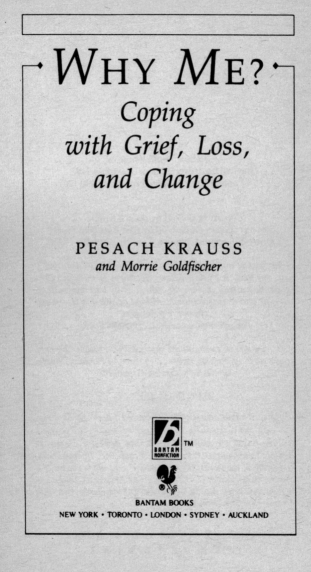

BANTAM BOOKS
NEW YORK · TORONTO · LONDON · SYDNEY · AUCKLAND

WHY ME?
A Bantam Nonfiction Book
Bantam hardcover edition/December 1988
Bantam paperback edition/April 1990

BANTAM NONFICTION *and the portrayal of a boxed "b" are*
trademarks of Bantam Books, a division of Bantam Double-
day Dell Publishing Group, Inc.

ISBN 0-553-28228-X

Published simultaneously in the United States and Canada

Bantam Books are published by Bantam Books, a division of
Bantam Doubleday Dell Publishing Group, Inc. Its trademark,
consisting of the words "Bantam Books" and the portrayal of a
rooster, is Registered in U.S. Patent and Trademark Office and
in other countries. Marca Registrada. Bantam Books, 666 Fifth
Avenue, New York, New York 10103.

PRINTED IN THE UNITED STATES OF AMERICA
OPM   10   9   8   7   6   5   4   3   2

To my wife Joan—
co-author of all that
is best in my life; to
our beloved children, Baruch, Hillel,
Jeremy and Nurit, Miriam,
David; and to Molly—
mother, grandmother, our inspiration.

A C K N O W L E D G M E N T S

I would like to thank those whose aid and support made this book possible: Neal Hirschfeld, for his early contributions to the book's concept and structure; Nat Sobel, my agent, for his invaluable assistance; Barbara Alpert, my editor, for her encouragement and guidance; The New York Board of Rabbis for having faith in selecting me to serve as chaplain at Memorial Sloan-Kettering Cancer Center; The Hospital Chaplaincy for encouraging me to write this book; fellow chaplains whose dedication to the patients daily inspires me; special gratitude to Reverend George Handzo, Protestant chaplain and brother in spirit and endeavor; and to all those patients and their families and my numerous congregants who have taught me so much and whose examples are a shining and guiding light for me.

"We know that every moment is a moment of grace, every hour an offering; not to share them would be to betray them. Our lives no longer belong to us alone; they belong to all who need us desperately."

—ELIE WIESEL, winner of
the 1986 Nobel Peace Prize,
in his acceptance speech

CONTENTS

INTRODUCTION

Why This Book Cried Out to Be Written

"Your pain is the breaking of the shell that encloses your understanding."

–KAHLIL GIBRAN

For the past six years I have served as a chaplain at Memorial Sloan-Kettering Cancer Center in New York, perhaps the most prestigious cancer hospital in the world. Hundreds of people, filled with hope and fear, pass through its portals daily.

Every day I relate intimately with patients struggling to survive and maintain their dignity. I have seen many courageous men and women marshal their emotional and spiritual resources to transcend intense pain, sorrow, anger, fear, and guilt. They have taught me a measure of life's wisdom that demands to be shared.

Patients under tremendous stress in a life-threatening illness search out the meaning of their lives. They often arrive at surprising answers (surprising because they are so obvious and so often overlooked) that apply to every human being—young, middle-aged, elderly—regardless of his or her health or station in life.

This enlightenment is by no means limited to chronically ill patients. I also serve as rabbi to a congregation of three hundred families. There I have seen new awareness evolve among men and women overwhelmed by problems of every description—family and work miseries, separation, job loss, midlife crisis, birth of a defective child, serious illness, death of a loved one.

I have long been aware that there is a hidden physical as well as spiritual force in the world, a power that heals our bodies and souls. When we are in touch with that power, we know it. It nourishes and elevates us. Call it God or whatever you will, it's there. The patients have made it real to me. Many have channeled into it. Isaiah, the prophet, experienced this power and cried out in amazement, "You will be lifted on eagles' wings and run and not tire."

Too many people make the mistake of judging life by its length rather than by its depth, by its problems rather than its promises. One is never too old or too ill to grow. Life is a series of peak moments. Such cherished moments—when we bring dignity upon ourselves, when we take a stand, when we experience love, when we open ourselves to others and to the world—give meaning to our lives.

The lesson is simple and profound. Each one of us is unique and irreplaceable. Every moment is precious, and not repeatable. Each person's life must have meaning—and each one must find it for himself. Life challenges us to discover our own specialness, our task, and to share with others.

Each day offers the opportunity and challenge for a new beginning. The wisdom of the Hebrew sages urges, "Be a partner with God in creation." And, as I see it, it behooves us to be more than a silent partner.

Since I began my chaplaincy at Memorial, my life has changed. I feel a tremendous power. I've shared these insights with my rabbinic colleagues at our national convention, in speeches before general audiences, and in sermons to my congregation. And my message of life and renewal has always been received with enthusiasm and gratitude.

When I enter a patient's room, I feel that I'm tapping into grief and anger, and I try to listen with what psychiatrists call the third ear. I have to hear what he's really saying, not just the words. My task is to help him draw upon his dormant or battered spiritual resources, to strengthen his hope and his courage and recall him to his dignity.*

In the hospital, patients search desperately for life's true and enduring values. And the values they discover or rediscover and the priorities they rearrange are the same ones that all of us struggle with in our attempts to lead richer, more fulfilling, more creative lives.

People everywhere are hurting and bewildered—which is why this book cried out to be written. In the following pages I share what I have learned. Although I serve in a cancer hospital, this is not a book about death and dying. In fact, it is just the opposite. It aims to tell how we can transcend the inevitable suffering and tragedy we all encounter to use and enjoy our sacred gift of life to the fullest. I hope it will bring comfort, guidance, and real understanding of life's meaning. That is my purpose in writing it.

---

*For convenience and clarity, I have used the masculine gender in many places throughout this book, though my intention is to speak to both men and women equally.

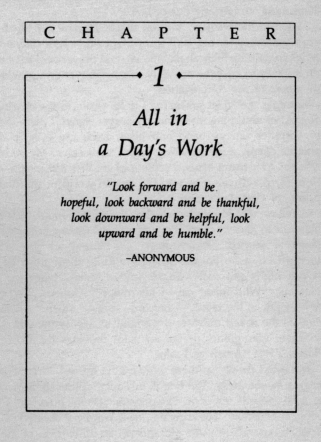

CHAPTER

· 1 ·

All in a Day's Work

*"Look forward and be
hopeful, look backward and be thankful,
look downward and be helpful, look
upward and be humble."*

–ANONYMOUS

This day starts like so many others. I have no inkling that it will bring my most challenging confrontation.

The alarm clock rings. Bleary-eyed, I see the luminescent dial outlined in the darkness: 5:45 A.M. I rush to depress the alarm lever so that my wife, Joan, will not be disturbed. Closing my eyes, I whisper, "Thank you, God, for returning my soul." I am alive another day. My daily prayer on awakening nudges me out of bed.

Down to the kitchen. A quick snack, prepare my lunch, grab the bag with my *tallit* (prayer shawl), *tefillin* (phylacteries containing Biblical quotations), and prayer books. I am on my way to my prework daily *minyan* (prayer group) with members of my congregation.

Entering the small sanctuary, I drop a coin in the charity box. After wrapping myself in my prayer shawl, I place the phylacteries on my hand and head, close my eyes, and breathe deeply. Fatigue slowly begins to dissolve. My body relaxes. As tension eases, I settle into another dimension—from secular-driven time into the eternal world of spiritual peace, of God, faith, and trust.

A fellow worshipper approaches the prayer stand, raises his voice in ancient chant. Prayers of thanksgiving begin the order of service. *"Baruch attah . . .* Praised are you, O loving God, who enables his creatures to distinguish between night and day." We respond, "Amen," after each blessing. "Who made me in his image." "Amen." "Who gives sight to the blind." I touch my eyes. "Amen." "Who clothes the naked, releases the bound, raises up the downtrodden, who guides us on our path, provides for all our needs . . ." "Amen and Amen."

My mind dwells on these words. I am moved. Tiredness begins to ebb away. The tide is in—deep calling to deep—and I try to ride the crest. The prayers raise me on wings of song, meditation, thanksgiving, awe. Words of divine wisdom, thousands of years old and yet so up-to-date, of the Bible, the psalmists, and of the ancient sages of the Talmud ring me round. Daily concerns, problems, worries, take on a new perspective.

The worship completed, I remove my phylacteries, fold my prayer shawl, and greet my congregants. "Have a good day, do a mitzvah (good deed)." They respond, "You too, Rabbi." Walking quickly to the exit, I kiss the mezuzah (religious symbol containing biblical quotations written on parchment) on the doorpost, murmur, "God give me strength," and am off.

Driving from Brooklyn to Manhattan each morning, coping with the inevitable early-morning traffic crunches, I've become a skilled broken-field runner, dodging the obstacles, scooting into the openings. After a trip that can take an hour, I arrive at Memorial Sloan-Kettering Cancer Center and search for a parking place. The time is now 7:45 A.M.

Rockefeller Institute and Hospital, with its large dome and gardens, is across the street, and the massive New York Hospital is on the other corner. No place to park. Cars are ticketed by an aggressive traffic squad. But I'm okay. I head for the empty space next to the No Parking sign. It's just right for me. I place my handicapped permit (a daily reminder of my own pain) against the windshield, angle the car next to the curb, and park.

I clip my ID badge, "Chaplain Rabbi Pesach Krauss," to my jacket pocket, pick up my briefcase, step out of the car, and start off on the run. All the residue of weariness evaporates like the morning mist before the warming sun of prayer and the mitzvah tasks that await me. There's always a keen sense of excitement. I never know what's in store for me each day, who I will meet and who I may help encourage—and who will reject my outreach.

Memorial Sloan-Kettering is an awesome and imposing place. The electrically controlled doors open at my approach. I wave to the security guard and hasten through the already bustling corridors to the computer room to pick up the daily printout of the Jewish patients. Carefully scanning each name, I make a mental note of the current patients who require another visit as well as the new patients to be seen.

It seems that the list grows longer each day and I wonder how I can cover all the patients. There are fourteen floors, each floor dealing with a different kind of cancer diagnosis and treatment. I pick up the patients' cards on which I will write my notes and am on my way.

My first stop is the small, spare, two-desk office that I share with Reverend George Handzo, the Protestant chaplain. After reading the notes and messages on the bulletin board, I pick up my tools—the beeper, the visitation cards with my name, the prayer cards, the red tabs to clip onto cards calling for special attention, the tiny books of Hebrew psalms, paper clips. With bulging pockets I am ready to start my rounds.

Before I begin, I duplicate four copies of the daily printout for the rabbinical students whom I'm training for hospital visitation of patients with catastrophic illnesses. The students, chosen from three Jewish seminaries, are each assigned a number of floors. I closely supervise their work. Reverend Handzo is training four Christian seminarians similarly.

Leaving the printouts for the students, I head for the Intensive Care Unit to see those most critically ill. From there I go to rooms where patients or family members have requested special visits. My assigned floors follow. As I arrive on each floor, I scan the list for patients scheduled for surgery. This is a most fearful and tense time for patients and their families.

The first room I visit is occupied by a new patient, a strong-featured, craggy, sixty-year-old man, a professor at a nearby university. He is having surgery for possible cancer of the bladder. His wife and son are at the bedside. As I enter the room, I take in the situation at a glance. The patient's feelings, his body language, the family's agitation, speak to me.

"Shalom, I'm Rabbi Pesach Krauss, the hospital chaplain. I've come to visit you. I see you are due for surgery this morning."

"Yes, Rabbi, I am glad to see you." I approach the patient's bed. Sensing his anxiety, I try to relate. "This is frightening,"

I say. "Oh, yes," he responds. "I'll admit it. I'm scared. Book learning isn't much help in this situation."

I reach out and touch his shoulder, letting him know I feel for his pain. "Who is your doctor?" He names him. "He's excellent," I assure him. "You have a very good surgeon." After a pause, I ask, "Would you like me to recite a prayer for you?" He answers, "Please, Rabbi, yes."

Holding the patient's hand, I recite the prayer in Hebrew with my eyes closed. My voice is soft but I try to keep it strong and upbeat. I ask the family to come closer. I translate:

"May the Almighty, our creator, our healer, bring you a speedy and complete healing. May He release His healing power within you, together with your will and courage and the support of your loved ones. May He grant wisdom to His messenger, the physician, to bring you along the way of health. *Y'varechecha* . . . may the Merciful One watch over you and bless you and sustain you with *chayim* (life), years, health, and *nachas* (spiritual pleasure)."

I breathe deeply. The patient closes his eyes during the prayer and, at the conclusion, holds on for a moment. The prayer impacts. He sheds a tear, opens his eyes. "Thank you, Rabbi," he says. "That helped me."

Not every patient responds this way to my approach. Some say, "No, thank you, Rabbi. Prayer is not my thing. I don't want to be a hypocrite." When this happens, I say, "May I then wish you health through the doctor's skill and the strength and support from your loved ones?" Very often, they answer, "That, I appreciate."

I turn to the wife and son and tell them that I must now visit other patients. I also tell them they may, if they wish, beep me when the attendant comes to take the patient for surgery.

In another room on that floor is a thirty-five-year-old woman who has undergone a biopsy for possible breast cancer. She has just heard the good news that her condition was benign. As I congratulate her and wish her well, my beeper sounds. The college professor's wife is calling. "Please come, Rabbi, the attendant has arrived."

I leave the woman and race down the corridor, entering the room just as the patient is being wheeled out. The wife and son are on either side of the stretcher, each grasping the patient's hand. We approach the holding room. The family members leave and I enter with the patient. I stay with him for a few minutes before he is taken to the operating room.

Later, between visits to other patients, I come to the waiting room and spend time with the wife and son, who are now awaiting word from the surgeon. I suggest reading psalms. I find that that can be helpful. I tell them they may beep me when they hear the operation is over. Then I will go to the recovery room and bring their love to the patient and the patient's love to them.

Waiting during a critical operation is excruciatingly painful, sheer hell. I've been through it. I know. And if I can bring some comfort, it makes my day.

And now back to the floor. There are other patients to visit. I check my cards. Next on the list is a very familiar name. Can it really be that one of the world's most famous scientists is in the room that I'm approaching?

I didn't know it then, but this patient was about to put me to my greatest test as a spiritual adviser.

• 2 •

Finding and
Opening Windows of
Hope

"It is plain that we exist for
our fellow men—in the first place for those upon whose
smiles and welfare our happiness depends, and next
for all those unknown to us personally
but to whose destinies we
are bound by the tie
of sympathy."

–ALBERT EINSTEIN

This day was bright and sunny but the shade-drawn private room was dimly lit and, at first, I didn't recognize a man whose name was a household word. He lay on his bed, partially hunched over, his gray hair rumpled, his face white, his hands limp at his side. I could see that he was seriously ill and deeply depressed.

When I introduced myself, he told me his name. I stared at him. Yes, this wan, emaciated, apathetic man really was the world-renowned scientist. How, I wondered to myself, can I give solace and comfort to a man of such erudition and achievement?

"How are you feeling today?" I asked him.

"Rabbi," he responded wearily, "I know my condition and I know I'm terminal. I have a blockage. It's very painful and my only future is greater pain. Oh, they'll try to ease the pain, but the road ahead is completely dark."

He paused, looked up at me, and said in a low but argumentative voice, "Tell me, Rabbi, what does God say about this?"

I stood there for a moment, not quite knowing how to continue. I felt that anything I said would have no effect. He was asking the universal and inevitable question—"Why me?"—and I was sure he knew all the answers as far as science and philosophy were concerned. We talked for a while and, when I left the room shortly thereafter, I felt that I had been challenged and had not been up to the test posed by a man of such stature.

When I visited him again, I decided I would reach out to him on just a plain human level of concern for his pain, feeling his anguish, just being there. Subsequently we had many opportunities for conversation, were quite open with each other, and became good friends.

It turned out that, despite his fame and frequent calls from colleagues all over the world, he was a lonely and tormented soul. His work had lost its punch and he pursued it listlessly. His wife and child were in their California home because he wanted to spare them the agony of seeing him waste away.

One day he touched bottom. "Pesach," he said, "you know my condition. It's hopeless. I'm all alone here. My outlook is only for greater pain and indignity. The quality of my life will only disintegrate. I'm thinking that while I still have my faculties and strength, suicide is the only rational act. What do you think? Should I commit suicide or not?"

I thought for a moment. I knew I had to be truthful

because he would recognize any dissimulation or falsehood. He would lose respect for me and our communication would end. "My own tradition," I answered, "maintains that every moment is precious, that life is a gift from God and only He can terminate it." I paused, and then plunged in. "But you know something, dammit, if I were in your situation, I just don't know. Maybe I, too, might think of a way out."

At these words he reached over and touched me. "Thank you for being honest. I appreciate that. There's nobody else I can talk to about that subject. Anyhow, I'm too much of a coward to commit suicide."

That was the conclusion of that conversation and the question of suicide never came up again.

I'm not a miracle worker. But perhaps having me alongside him at that desperate time helped strengthen his resolve. I think he had reached a crisis moment, and my relating to him on a level of genuine concern, listening very carefully to what he had to say, reaching out to shore up his dignity, gave him a feeling that he did have control and the time to do worthwhile things despite an almost hopeless situation.

I realized that he was suffering through a personal grief process of loss and letting go, an emotional torment felt by most patients dreading their possible imminent death. After all, their lives are to be terminated—and that's a very, very difficult fact to face, especially, perhaps, for this very famous man with such great responsibilities, so many projects still on his agenda.

The thought of leaving all that in addition to his family, his wife, his young child, was overpowering. Somehow I had to help him deal with it. I didn't try to gloss over the true seriousness of his situation. I was just there for him, searching for that elusive window of hope. But it had to be a realistic one, growing out of his own life.

When he spoke I listened carefully, trying to determine the message behind his words, trying to find an opening. I caught the sense of pride and accomplishment he had about his work. That was when I decided to ask him how he had overcome his most serious professional obstacles. Perhaps recalling his past strengths would help him focus on how to cope with and surmount his present crisis.

I said, "Were there any times in your research when you ran up against a brick wall?" Because so much depended on his answer to this pivotal question, I held my breath waiting for his reply.

He was silent for a moment, deep in thought. At last he spoke. "Oh, yes, I've had some real doozies, times when our country's defense was at stake, when most of the world was potentially involved. And I felt a heavy, heavy responsibility."

The conversation was going as I had hoped. "Well," I said, "how did you deal with those crises? What is your way of coping with major problems when they arise?"

"I'm not the kind that runs away from a fight," he said. "I'm a scientist. I gather all the facts, painstakingly review the given data, and realistically assess implications and the strengths and weaknesses of each situation. Then I pick the best choice and go full speed ahead."

"Did you face your personal problems in the same way?" I asked.

"You bet," he said. "I've had my share of personal problems and always handled them in a strong and rational way."

That was my cue. "Well, right now," I said, "you're facing what is surely the most difficult problem you've ever come up against. Maybe the strength and the creative intuitive grasp of a situation you showed when you found other solutions, perhaps where it seemed there were no solutions, where nobody else could find them, might be the kind of strength you can draw on today. Think about it. You've never ducked a tough assignment."

That got him thinking. To fortify his resolve further, I

asked about his web of associations, those who loved him, who respected him, who could give him support and strength at this crucial time.

"There's no question about it," he said. "I have a wonderful wife and helpmate who's been very devoted to me for many years."

"Are you able to talk freely with her and completely share your feelings?" I asked.

"Yes," he said, "but I've been trying to shield her."

"Is that why she's not here with you?"

"Yes, I can handle this best myself."

"How does that make you feel?" I asked him.

"Lonely as hell. I feel alone, frightened, and it's painful."

Then I said, "How do you think she feels, being so far away?"

"Well, I call her every night." He paused. "You know, you're right. She wants to be here near me. I sense it and hear it in her voice."

"To me," I said, "it seems it must be even worse for her, with her imagination running wild and picturing the worst. Do you think she's crying at this very moment?"

"It's quite possible, although she's very controlled. And I am too."

"For goodness sake," I said, "wouldn't it be good to cry sometime and release some of the terrible tension within you?"

He confided, "I'll admit to you, I have cried when nobody was around."

"That's no weakness," I told him. "Keeping all those feelings locked up inside you is like having the pressure build in a teakettle. Unless you let it escape, it will explode. Let it go."

Softly he said, "You're right" and began to sob. I came closer, held his hand as his body shook uncontrollably.

Later I told him not to be embarrassed by his tears in my presence, that he had gained strength by accepting support from another human being. I pointed out that scientists build their accomplishments upon the shoulders of others. "If you can borrow from others' achievements in the laboratory," I asked, "why not take now from someone who can support you in your need? As you take, you are truly giving to someone as well."

I believe that that realization helped him decide that he wanted to go home and spend his time with his wife and child. He became aware that that was where he would gain tremendous support and strength and also give strength. He began looking forward eagerly to spending the hours, days, weeks, maybe months ahead in a close sharing relationship with his family.

Before he left the hospital, I challenged him again. I said, "This is going to be a very difficult and painful question to answer. Perhaps you might not want to deal with it. But I'm going to ask you anyway. What has cancer taught you?"

I had caught him unawares. Pensive, he was silent for several long moments. "You know," he finally said, "it has taught me a number of things. That I'm not so high and mighty. Not to be so arrogant, because I don't know it all. Nor am I in complete control of my life and what happens to it." He paused, then continued.

"However, in the most important sense, I guess I'm still in control because my attitude makes all the difference in the world as to how I leave this world. That's one thing I've learned.

"I've learned something else. That life is precious, that every moment has to count. I feel it when I get up in the morning and when I have a day without pain. It's amazing, it's like I'm reborn every day, recapturing the wonder of another day. I feel as though there's an inner light shining. It's like—as you put it—the flow of God's mercy, or maybe nature's mercy, and it brings warmth like the sun's rays."

He pointed to a red rose in a vase on the windowsill. "See that flower? I look at that rose like I've never seen a rose before. I'm so sensitive to its color, the light and shadows playing on it, to its texture, and the way it's formed. What a marvelous, exquisite work of art, what a miracle it is! And I smell the fragrance of the rose—and it just fills my body."

We looked into each other's eyes for a moment. Then, smiling, he continued. "I've really learned how precious time is. How wonderful love is, too—the love of my child, the love of my wife. Oh, I've always known it, but I was always too busy to really appreciate it. Now it's central, and fresh, like that flower. I know who my true friends are and those I won't bother with at all because there is so little time."

I told him that perhaps he had gained a different perspective and a different set of priorities. He agreed.

"I know how I'm going to spend my time," he said. "For one thing, I'll be involved in the creative end of my science. I can't do it in the lab anymore but, person to person, I can do a great deal. You've seen me phoning, the others calling me. Keeping in contact, reaching out to others. That's where it counts."

I nodded agreement and he continued.

"I guess what I'm trying to say is that a number of values have suddenly become clear in my life. Things I've never stopped to think about, even in my work. Creation is one of them. I didn't come into my knowledge on my own. I had to build on the foundation of giants. And I wish to find some time to give back to the world some newly created works to show my gratitude for all the things given to me.

"Another thing I've learned is the joy of just being open to experience the wonders of the world, its beauties, and its mysteries. I guess when you're hit with something and there's no way out, you have to find a way in, to live in greater depth. I suppose I should have lived my whole life that way, but I never would have been able to if I hadn't the insights that come with pain and terror. But there are so many things surfacing that are just marvelous. I want to thank you for everything you've helped me to see. And a lot of what I've learned is because you really challenged me—and you've been here for me and with me."

From then on he was dynamized. His room became the busiest in the whole hospital. The telephone rang constantly with calls from all over the country.

"What are they calling you for?" I asked.

"For recommendations, for insights, for suggestions. There's so much to be done, so much to be achieved."

One day, when I visited him, he said, "Pesach, my colleagues tell me that I don't know what I've done for them, that my courage and resolution in facing my illness is an inspiration to them. That means a great deal to me."

When the nurses came into the room to do what they had to do, he wasn't even aware they were there. A sense of tremendous energy, excitement, and, yes, happiness, pervaded that room.

The shades were always up. The room was brilliantly sunlit by day. And he told me how, at night, he looked out at the cars along the highway, their headlights illuminating the evening, and the twinkling lights of the bridge spanning the river, and their reflection on the water. He saw all this and more—and he was open to every experience.

There came the day when he told me he was going home.

"What are you going to do when you get there?" I asked.

"First, I'm going to be with my child. He's ten years old and needs his father around. We're going to go fishing and spend a lot of time doing things together."

"Are you going to tell him about your situation?" I asked.

"Yes, definitely," he said. "It's not important that I'm a famous scientist. It matters more that I have a deep and honest relationship with my son. And he will remember me for that. We're going to make every moment count."

When he left, he was no longer isolated from his family or his colleagues. And perhaps he was living in his greatest depth. He had a whole new perspective on what he was going to do with his remaining moments. Beyond the triumphs of his scientific achievements, he now had triumphs in human relationships. He would be remembered not only for his brilliance, as important as it was, but as much for his humanity.

As I saw it, he had transcended his illness. He had gone through his odyssey of terror and denial and depression and then, walking through the valley of the shadow of death as in Psalm Twenty-three, he had found a light shining at the end of the dark valley. That is, he came to accept his situation and deal with it as he had always done with problems in his past, logically, seeing where he had to go and how to get there, and finding also other options—windows of hope—that had been closed to him before and were now open.

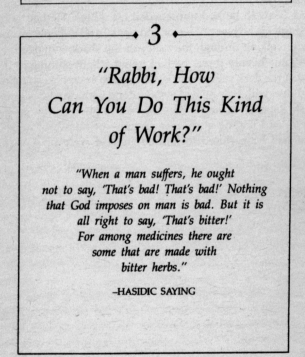

CHAPTER

• 3 •

"Rabbi, How Can You Do This Kind of Work?"

"When a man suffers, he ought not to say, 'That's bad! That's bad!' Nothing that God imposes on man is bad. But it is all right to say, 'That's bitter!' For among medicines there are some that are made with bitter herbs."

–HASIDIC SAYING

When a person enters a hospital and becomes a patient, he loses his identity. His clothes are taken from him, a plastic band is placed around his hand, and he becomes, in a sense, a number. Doctors come in, poking around; nurses perform indignities; he becomes completely dependent on others for his every need; and he loses control over his very being.

When there is a life-threatening illness, the patient's priorities are all disrupted. The physical pain and even more intense spiritual and emotional suffering are terrifying and overwhelming. At Memorial Sloan-Kettering Cancer Center, where I serve as the first full-time Jewish chaplain, I minister, day in and day out, to the sick and dying, and to their loved ones.

When people meet me, they invariably ask, "Rabbi, how can you do this kind of work?" They cannot comprehend why I would be willing to take on the burden of counseling cancer patients, many of whom are terminally ill. In fact, virtually all my colleagues advised against my accepting the position. They warned that I would be subjecting myself to unbearable emotional overload and eventual burnout.

Frankly, before accepting the chaplaincy, I wrestled with the prospect, feeling inadequate, wondering if I really had something special to offer. I looked at what I had been through, remembering my own searing pain, anger, guilt, isolation, sense of abandonment, all the anguish I experienced when my first wife died of cancer.

I asked myself, "Can I subject myself to this again with so many patients?" After deep soul-searching, I decided that, having gone through the valley of the shadow of death, perhaps I could empathize with, understand, and relate to what the patients were feeling, and help them open windows of hope.

I've never regretted my decision and I would not trade my job for any other in the world. It's true that dealing with men and women suffering from cancer can be heartrending. It is extremely demanding, difficult, and challenging work. Many are the days when I leave the hospital feeling like I've been through a spiritual and emotional wringer. My loving wife, Joan, understands when I come home sometimes too dis-

pirited and upset to eat dinner. She encourages me to talk it
out. Later I feel better and strengthened.

The day I first walked into the hospital was the day of my
spiritual and emotional awakening. I had finally arrived. I
felt at home. I hadn't known it before, but I soon came to
realize that I had been preparing for this role all of my
rabbinic and academic career. Now, at long last, I felt secure
and sure of myself. Despite the warnings of my colleagues, I
did not become emotionally overloaded or burned out. On
the contrary, my wells of energy and creativity were replen-
ished. The immense challenge of working at Sloan-Kettering
energized and excited me and released my creativity.

This creativity has spilled over into my personal life and
into my work as rabbi of the Kings Highway Jewish Center
in Brooklyn, New York, which I also serve as spiritual leader.
Today I am dynamized. I start early, keep up a brisk pace
during the day, and often push on late into the evening. But I
am seldom tired. In fact, I feel more refreshed, more productive, and more creative than I ever felt in my thirty-eight
years as a rabbi.

Before I became a chaplain at Sloan-Kettering, I'd often
visit hospitals as part of my routine rabbinical duties. But it
was not the same. My conversations with patients were
mundane, superficial, often mere exercises in going through
the motions. When I dealt with people who were the victims
of lesser illnesses or injuries, our talks seldom went beyond
scratching the surface. The protective masks were still in
place. At times, so meaningless were the words—both theirs
and mine—that I'd sometimes pinch myself to keep from
drowsing off.

Now I'm wide awake—all the time. That's because at
Sloan-Kettering I counsel people who are suffering from
cancer. People who are battling cancer drop their masks.
And when they do, I'm right there with them. With my
patients now, I get into the "guts" of it all, what they are
really feeling and thinking deep down inside.

I become a part of the most intimate flow of their lives, their fears, guilts, disappointments, and dreams. The stories they tell exposing their innermost lives are extraordinarily revealing and moving. A dramatist could have an inexhaustible supply of material for writing plays just by being in my shoes.

My reward, however, is much greater than just the vicarious experience of listening to other people's life stories. The nurture I receive from my patients, the courage, the appreciation, the opening up and sharing of the most intimate feelings and events, the realization of the fragility and brevity of life—including my own—all these bring sharply into focus my own everyday blessings and clarify my own priorities.

These realizations have carried over into my synagogue tasks. My sermons have become more personal. I stress these priorities when I speak to members of my congregation who face these same issues in different ways. My sermons are enriched by the illustrations drawn from the life experiences of patients at Sloan-Kettering.

These are true stories of courage and faith; the reordering of priorities; facing disappointments, illness, pain, and death and, at times, great moments of transcending. I listen with my heart to those who are reaching out in their times of greatest need. Where else could I possibly find more stirring, more touching, more inspiring examples of human struggle?

But, above all, I feel that the greatest reward from my hospital work is just being there. Being needed when there's suffering. The thanks I receive with a tear or a squeeze of the hand. When a patient greets me with a smile and says, "Rabbi, so good to see you. You don't know what courage and comfort and consolation you've given me." These events make my day, brighten my life, lighten my own burden. They enhance my feelings of worth in this world. They give strength and substance to my sense of self-esteem.

"Rabbi, how can you do the kind of work that you do?"

The answer is that I feed my *"neshama."* *"Neshama"* is a Hebrew word meaning "soul" or the "breath of God." As I listen to a patient, and he knows that I am truly listening, he grows in dignity because somebody cares. I give him that sense of recapturing his dignity. And he gives *me* dignity in return. And thus my own *"neshama"* is fed and sustained.

This interchange can work only if we do not allow ourselves to become depressed and thus turn away from our higher potential. Depression is a pernicious illness that can ultimately disarm our immune system and even destroy us. Joy, on the other hand, can have an opposite effect.

Recent medical research bears this out. Herbert Spector, a neurophysiologist at the National Institutes of Health, says, "The ancients knew that the patient's attitude was very important to his recovery, but modern medicine wrote it off as trivial. The new research makes it clear. Attitudes can matter."

Among those reporting similar findings is Paul J. Rosch, M.D., president of the American Institute of Stress. "It is increasingly evident that the mind and emotions have a profound influence on immune-system function and there is a continuing dialogue between these closely related structures," Dr. Rosch says. "If distress can lower immune defenses, it is likely that there are opposing states of mind or mood that bolster them . . . implying a vast untapped potential for self-healing."

If, as the psalmist sings, we "serve God in rejoicing," our spirits soar. When we channel into certain positive values our lives are enriched. It isn't necessary to rejoice only in giving, acting, doing, or recreating something worthwhile. We can also benefit by receiving, just opening ourselves up, not doing anything except experiencing and being thankful for and rejoicing in the beauty of the universe, esthetics, art, health, family, love.

And, on the profoundest level, even where there is

suffering and loss, we can learn to accept these painful circumstances and use them creatively to delve deeper into the substrata of what our life is all about. All these ways of finding out our own meaning in the universe can be opportunities for the greatest growth.

As I see it, we should not speak only in terms of "depth" psychology, but of "height" psychology as well, reaching not only more deeply into ourselves but also reaching up beyond ourselves to help others. To paraphrase Goethe: "If you take people as they are, you make them worse than they are. If you take people as they could be, you make them achieve what they would be."

The issue for me has never been how I can do the work I do. Instead, these are the questions I ask myself: "How can I help a person with a catastrophic illness recover his self-image and cope? Even in the waning days of his life, how can I help him find real purpose and meaning so that he can transcend his illness, live in his greatest depth, and attain his greatest height?"

Whether we are seriously ill or in the pink of health, all of us are searching for meaning in one way or another. More than the drive for sex, the drive for wealth, or the drive for power, it is the drive for meaning that impels and gives direction to life.

When I meet a patient in the hospital, I always feel like I am meeting myself. That's because every one of us—atheist, agnostic, or believer—must confront the core issues of our existence throughout life and especially in times of adversity: Who am I? For what purpose was I placed on this earth? Where is my dignity? What is my self-worth? What am I doing with the time left to me? How do I transcend my suffering even when there seems no way out? These are the issues I grapple with when I'm with my patients. And these are the issues I shall explore in this book.

At Sloan-Kettering, afflictions force the patients to discard their masks and face these basic issues head-on. Some do it sooner. Some do it later, and some never. For some patients it takes a while to open up, drop their defenses, and express what's really on their minds. When they come to the hospital, having been diagnosed with cancer, they feel ashamed and inferior. They see themselves as incomplete human beings and damaged goods. Worst of all, because of the stigma that is attached to this particular disease, they often feel abandoned by friends and family.

"Why me, Rabbi?" they will ask. "Dammit, *why me*! How could God do this to me? *Why me?*"

There is no easy answer to these questions. This is a time when people are desperately grasping for hope. Some even bargain with God, with no limits on what they will barter for restoration of their health.

Perhaps you've heard the apocryphal story of the atheist mountain climber who lost his grip as he approached the summit but managed to grab a branch that stopped his fall. Holding on for dear life, he called out, "God, you haven't been part of my life and I didn't even think you existed. But I need help now. If you can help me, I'll be your follower. Please, God, answer me if you are there!" Suddenly a loud and clear voice responded, "My son, I know you haven't been faithful, but here I am. Do you trust me?" The man answered, "Oh, yes, I do now." The voice continued, "Then trust in me and let go." There was a pause. "Is there anyone else up there?" the man shouted.

Every time I enter the room of the terminally ill, I feel that I'm hanging over that chasm with the patient. I empathize with his feelings of sadness, inadequacy, deep puzzlement, and rage. What can I say? How can I help?

This is not a time to be intellectual and to reason with him. Instead, you must be there with him in his grief, to help him face his heavy emotional load, help him work out his mourning for the loss of his health. Once he sees that you're open with him, that you understand where he is, that you're not going to just "make nice," then you can help him go through the shadow of the sorrow his pain has brought him.

If the patient is ready, I will challenge him to take responsibility for his life and try to help him gain a positive perspective. Simply put, the perspective is that loss, difficult as it is to bear, is part of ongoing life. If we don't grasp that basic fact while young, we have to learn it later.

Life is not a fairy tale where the poor squire wins the princess's hand, marries her, and lives happily ever after. It just doesn't happen that way. And, if life entails a series of losses, we must learn to use these losses creatively, not only to cope, but to transcend and, beyond that, to grow. That means developing a solid sense of values to help us grow.

People who come to this hospital feel that somebody has pulled the rug out from under them. They're still trying to retrieve their equilibrium and catch their breath. I understand what it's like to have the rug pulled out from under you. And I understand it better than most.

I understand this, quite simply, because of what happened to me.

• 4 •

Learning
I Could Be Whole Even If
Part of Me Is
Missing

*"Experience is valuable only
when it has brought suffering and
when the suffering has left its
mark upon both body
and mind."*

– ANDRÉ MAUROIS

When I was growing up in Cincinnati, I was run over by a streetcar. My right leg was so badly injured that it had to be amputated just below the knee.

I was three years old when the accident occurred.

The toes on my left foot were mashed and mangled and the doctors wanted to amputate that leg as well. Surgical procedures were far less advanced sixty years ago than they are today, and it was ... such extensive damage. ...

My father, however, re... operation and, thank God, h... moved a couple of toes and left tw... the leg itself was saved. Many years ... the doctors had pressed to amputat... ...ny father had become so distraught that he ... ...own a hospital corridor, screaming wildly, and ... ... commit suicide by throwing himself from an upper-fl... window. A police officer who happened to be nearby wrestled him to the ground and kept him restrained until he was able to compose himself.

As for the accident itself, I don't remember a great deal; it all happened so many years ago. My parents had come to this country only a few years earlier from Russia, and we were living in a rickety, roach-infested apartment house near the streetcar tracks. One day the front gate had inadvertently been left open and I ran out and up the block to visit a cousin who lived nearby. That was when the streetcar hit me.

From that point on, my recollections are mercifully vague. I don't remember the moment of impact, nor do I remember the pain. As for the trip to the hospital or the operations that were performed, my mind, to this day, is a blank. I can remember walking on crutches after the surgery and I can also remember being fitted for an artificial leg.

In moments of terrible tragedy, the mind sometimes erases the major details of a traumatic event and rivets itself to the minor ones. For some reason, my most vivid bedside recollection of my father during my convalescence is of the spearmint gum he would always chew and the fresh, minty fragrance it left on his breath.

As devastating as the accident was for me, it was, in some ways, even worse for my parents. They were poor immigrants, and because of some painful setbacks they had already suffered in life, they became convinced that God had child, my mother had been unwanted. run off when she was very young, her mother married, and she herself had been sent to live with her grandmother. For all practical purposes, my mother was brought up believing she was an orphan.

My father's early life had also been rough. He had been a poor tailor in Russia and had fallen in love with a beautiful girl from a wealthy family. But, in the old country, this girl was considered above his station. Ultimately, because of my father's impoverished background and his humble circumstances, the girl's family rejected him as a suitor. He never fully recovered from the turndown.

But the most crushing blow of all for both of my parents— and this was something I did not learn until many years later, after my father's death—was that before coming to this country from Russia in 1920, my parents had had another child. A little girl. She had fallen ill with some disease that was rampant in Russia and had died. At her death she was three years old. That was exactly my age when the streetcar hit me.

Given the loss of their first child and the crippling of their second, it was all too understandable that my parents would think God had turned against them. And, sadly, in their anguish over the tragedies that had befallen their children, my parents turned against each other.

I would hear them arguing and accusing. "Why did you leave the gate open?" my father would shout angrily. "I couldn't help it!" my mother would shout back. "I was busy. I didn't know he had gotten out. One minute he was there. The next minute he was gone. It wasn't my fault!" Sometimes the arguments would turn especially ugly, and I remember my mother bursting into tears. She would cry and run to me. I would cry, and my father would continue to shout.

At heart my parents were really good and decent people, filled with enormous love for me, and there was never a moment when I was not aware of how deep that love was. But my parents were simple people and there were many things in life they just couldn't comprehend. After my accident they were consumed by grief and guilt and shame over my leg, and for many years thereafter our home saw a great deal of strife and tension.

As a boy I attended the School for Crippled Children in Cincinnati. Since everyone at this school was handicapped, I wasn't that self-conscious about my artificial leg. In fact, one of my earliest and most gratifying recollections is of a photograph of me when I was a pupil there. I must have been climbing a pole in a playground when the picture was taken, for in it you can see me at the very top, clinging with both hands and smiling triumphantly. Standing at the bottom of the pole is another crippled child, who is looking up at me with tremendous admiration. That photo of me, showing me having made it to the top, is something I still treasure to this day.

One day, when I was seven or eight years old, the principal of the School for Crippled Children called me to his office. When I entered, he placed a stool in front of me.

"Pesach," the principal said, "can you jump over this stool?"

In one quick movement I made the leap to the other side, and turned to him, grinning.

The principal smiled. "Pesach," he said, "I think you're ready to leave us. It's time for you to transfer to public school."

The move to public school marked my first brush with the real world. In the School for Crippled Children I had been sheltered. Everyone in the school was disabled in one way or another, so I never felt different. But in public school I *was* different. I was not like the other boys and girls. I was the one with the artificial leg, the one with the limp, and I became very self-conscious about my impediment.

I was very eager to compete with the other kids, particularly in athletics, but I was also terrified that they might see my artificial leg and make fun of me. For that reason, whenever we played baseball or basketball or volleyball, I always wore long pants. After play and in the locker room, I would never shower, because I would have had to reveal my artificial leg. Although the kids all knew that I wore one, my shame was so great that I couldn't bear to let them see it.

Later, after school, I would go home and remove my prosthesis so I could soak my leg. When I was playing, particularly in warm weather, the scar tissue was easily damaged and my leg would become very sore. But this was something I would never dare acknowledge to my class-mates.

Once, I came home after a baseball game and was sitting on a cot in our living room. My leg had become irritated after playing, so I had removed my artificial limb and placed it on the floor, next to the cot. Suddenly, without prior warning, one of my friends appeared at the screen door. He had decided to pay me a surprise visit. But when I saw him, I became hysterical. I was terrified that he would see my artificial leg, and I began screaming, frantically, for my mother to rush into the living room and take the prosthesis away.

One of the things that made my shame and anxiety among my classmates so much greater was that my parents tried so hard to shelter me. So much guilt and embarrassment did they feel about my leg that they projected those feelings on me, and I took them to heart. After all, these were my parents talking, and if they felt this way about my disability, it was only natural that I should begin to feel guilty and ashamed in my own right.

I especially remember my father lecturing me that I was special, not like everyone else, and that because of my condition, I was never going to have to do any strenuous physical labor. "When you grow up," he would tell me, "you will do something professional. You will use your mind, not your body."

One time when I was about ten, a young neighbor in our building was selling magazine subscriptions. He was recruiting young boys in the neighborhood to go around door-to-door to solicit new customers. I volunteered to work for him. When my father found out about my new job, he became livid. "You shouldn't be going around selling magazines!" he scolded. "It's beneath your dignity. Besides, with your foot, it's just too much of a strain. I never want you to do that again."

Since my family was so adamant about not allowing me to work, I had to seek out other ways to validate my self-worth and give vent to my innate need to compete. Athletics became my passion, and I played sports with a vengeance.

In grade school I went out for the volleyball team. In spite of my artificial leg, I was a spark plug, running around the court like a madman, diving to make this shot or that one. Wherever the ball was, that's where I'd be. Looking back, I realize I was constantly trying to prove to myself and my whole-body teammates that, despite my handicap, I was as good as or even superior to them.

The problem, however, was that no matter how fast I ran or how high I jumped or how many homers I hit or how well I fielded, I could never be as good as the other kids. I was always a step behind. I was good, but I could never be *as* good. After a vigorous game of softball or volleyball, my leg would get sore, and I would come home limping. Sometimes, I would have to stay in bed for days.

I worshipped the ideal of a perfect body. I didn't realize it then, but in continually comparing myself with the other kids, in trying to be as good as they were, I was setting an impossible goal. And since I could never reach that goal, I always felt inferior. And tremendously resentful.

Years later, when I was a counselor in a summer camp, I shared a bunk with a young doctor who noticed that at

bedtime I would take off my prosthesis and push it underneath the bed so that even he shouldn't see it.

One day he told me that he had never seen me in the lake
and wondered if I had ever gone swimming. Somewhat
shamefacedly I told him that I didn't know how to swim and
couldn't face up to removing my prosthesis in front of the
children.

The doctor was an understanding and encouraging person
and at night, when everyone was asleep, he taught me how
to swim. When I was proficient, he said to me, "Pesach, why
don't you try swimming during the day?" I had thought
about it and decided to give it a try.

It was very difficult for me at first. I went into the lake
before the children came and, when I came out, covered my
foot with a towel. But I swam and it was great. Finally I got
up the courage to splash around with the kids. I was
partially released. Later I overcame another hurdle—I was
able to play tennis in short pants.

Because I felt inferior physically, I somehow convinced
myself that I was also inferior intellectually. In school, other
kids got A's or A minuses; my grades were never better than
average. Odd as it sounds, since I'm now a rabbi, I was even
an academic dud in Hebrew school. The white-bearded rabbi
once berated me in front of the entire class. "Krauss!" he
snapped. "You're not going to amount to anything." My
inferiority complex affected all the areas of my life. Socially,
because of my disability, I held myself back for many, many
years. I never even held a girl to dance with until I was
nineteen years old.

From my present perspective, I realize that I was searching
for my self-dignity, and it seemed to me that the way to
attain that status was to be a hero. To be the best. If I could be
a hero, I reasoned, then I could surmount my great feelings
of shame because of my disability and my awkwardness. If I
could be a hero, I would no longer feel inferior like a
nothing, a zero. But as long as I kept trying to compete with

the other kids—in ways that I simply couldn't compete—I would never attain my objective. I couldn't see it at the time, but I had locked myself into a perpetually self-defeating proposition. I was like the mythical king Sisyphus, who was doomed forever to roll uphill a great, heavy stone which always rolled right back down again.

But then, in high school, something happened that changed my life. In my freshman year I decided to go out for the gymnastics team.

I picked gymnastics because it was a sport in which none of my friends would be competing with me. They were all busy playing baseball. If I worked and trained hard enough in gymnastics, my disability would not inhibit me. And since my friends weren't into that activity, I would not always be measuring myself against them.

I threw myself into my new sport with fervor. Every day after school I would practice on the ropes, the rings, and the parallel bars. I never breathed a word to my parents about this new extracurricular activity; if they had found out, they undoubtedly would have put a stop to it. Had I taken a bad spill, I could have broken my artificial leg . . . or even fractured my good one.

My parents, who had pampered and sheltered me so tenaciously all these years, would have been furious if they found out what I was up to. At night, in my room, I would secretly record my aspirations in a diary. To make the team, to win a meet, to earn a letter—these were the things I longed for.

I remember one important all-state meet in which I competed. For weeks I had practiced an especially difficult dismount from the parallel bars, one in which I catapulted to a handstand on two bars, shifted all my weight to one bar, then pushed off, flew through the air, and landed right side up on the mat below. This particular dismount was extremely dangerous, and I wasn't certain I was going to use it on the day of the meet. In fact, to be perfectly honest, I was afraid to perform it. However, when I got up to do my routine, our team was lagging in points, and I realized I would have to use my special dismount if we were to have any chance of winning. So, as I came to the end of my routine, I chanced it.

I remember going up in the air, then letting go and reaching over to grab the other bar. For a moment, I just teetered there, my body swaying as I held on to that one bar. Sweat was pouring down my arms, slickening my palms and fingers. At that moment, hanging there suspended, I wasn't sure whether I would fall off or regain control. And as I began to sway, I could hear a collective gasp from all the people in the audience. They were holding their breath, waiting to see whether I would make it or flop to the floor in defeat.

Up on the bars I gritted my teeth. With all the strength that I could muster, I managed to steady myself and regain control of my legs. Then, pointing my toes skyward, I pushed off, propelled my body high into the air, and arched to the floor in an upright position. My landing was flawless.

The entire arena exploded with applause . . . and I won first prize in the state meet.

First prize!

Without question, that was one of the most exhilarating and joyous moments of my youth. I had done exactly what I had dreamed of doing. No longer was it just some idle schoolboy fantasy that I had scribbled in my diary. I had done it, and I had done it for real. And it wasn't just that I was a somebody. I was the best. A hero. Not merely as good as everyone else, but better. Because of my prowess at gymnastics, I was elected captain of the team in my junior year. In my senior year my classmates voted me class treasurer. I also won an athletic scholarship to college.

Yet, I must tell you, that as satisfying as that victory at the state meet was, there was another moment in those early years that was even more memorable. It happened in my sophomore year, when I first learned that I had officially made the school gymnastics team. There I was, walking down the hallway of my high school and into my homeroom class in that wonderful bulky red wool sweater with that huge, beautiful, glorious white letter "H" for Hughes High stitched to my chest. My letter! As I stepped into my classroom, my heart was bursting with pride.

Inside the classroom, the other kids stopped their chatter and turned to stare at me. Krauss, the kid with the gimpy leg . . . What was that he was wearing? A hush came over the room. And then an amazing thing happened.

In unison, all my classmates rose. They began to clap their hands. Softly at first. Then louder. And they cheered.

I'm not ashamed to tell you that on that day, standing there in front of my classmates, the tears I cried were the sweetest tears of all.

For the first time I had a glimmer that I could be a whole person even if part of me is missing.

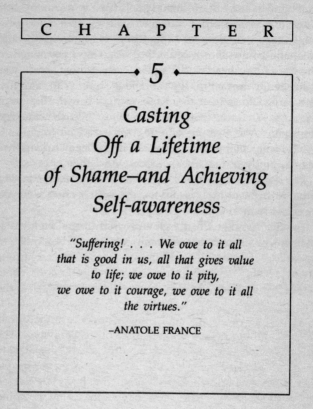

CHAPTER

• 5 •

Casting Off a Lifetime of Shame—and Achieving Self-awareness

"Suffering! . . . We owe to it all that is good in us, all that gives value to life; we owe to it pity, we owe to it courage, we owe to it all the virtues."

–ANATOLE FRANCE

If, as in a movie, my story could have abruptly ended with that wonderfully joyous classroom scene, all would have been well and good. But real life, as we all know, does not compartmentalize itself so easily or remain permanently contained by such neat and happy endings. Nothing is forever. Real life is a continuous process of setbacks and victories, struggles and breakthroughs, and my own battles with feelings of inferiority because of my artificial leg continued to plague me for many, many years thereafter.

Making the gymnastics team, winning that letter and being elected captain—all of that proved to me that I could excel and compete outwardly. But inwardly I continued to wrestle with a sense of inadequacy. Deep down inside was there really anything special about me? Who am I, I wondered. What is my purpose on this earth? And what could I possibly hope to contribute to my fellow man, given my obvious physical limitation? As I advanced into adulthood, I still had not come to terms with a deep-seated sense of being incomplete, inferior, damaged goods.

Two encounters, however, had a profound and lasting impact on the way I perceived myself. Both of them occurred some years after I had become a rabbi.

The first was a group therapy program that I attended at Boston University, where I was doing graduate studies in pastoral counseling. We were placed in the Massachusetts Mental Health Hospital, a subsidiary of the Harvard School of Medicine. Each day we met with and counseled the mental patients.

As part of the program, I was required to undergo six weeks of group therapy sessions with other clergymen. The sessions were intense—ninety minutes a day, five days a week, six weeks straight. In the beginning of these groups, there was a lot of psychological "junk" that had to be cleared out of the way—wrestling for power to see who would control the group, petty jealousies, hidden agendas, things that get in the way of people opening up and being honest with one another.

But after you're together with each other long enough, the masks start to crack and crumble. You no longer need the old defenses, and anything goes. A bond of trust is built up, and pretty soon you start to touch on the important issues that are really troubling people.

I had never participated in a group therapy encounter

before, and during the first few sessions I was utterly amazed at the intimate secrets that people were willing to reveal about themselves. A minister who had been placed in charge of a man's dormitory at a university confessed to the group that he was a homosexual. "I haven't been able to share this with anybody," the minister admitted. He said it matter-of-factly, yet all of us couldn't help but notice the tear in his eye. "If I did," he explained, "I'd lose my position with the church."

Another minister, who had been married a number of years, made what, to him, was a shocking revelation when he told us that he absolutely hated—of all things—peas! "I don't like peas," he said, and then, more emphatically, he shouted to all of us: "Dammit, I don't like peas!" It turned out that he had always been afraid to tell his wife that he hated peas. Whenever she made peas for dinner, this minister would eat them, even though he loathed them, rather than antagonize his wife. The real issue was not peas, but the minister's timidity.

We all go along with one thing or another, and if we believe that someone has power over us, we're very much afraid to reveal what we think and how we feel. As a result, our whole sense of dignity is lowered. We feel like less of a person. And that was what had happened to this minister, who was so fearful of confronting his wife with the fact that he hated peas.

Still another minister's revelation was even more melodramatic.

As he started to talk about his childhood, he suddenly burst into hysterical laughter. For ten minutes he cackled uproariously, without interruption. There was something almost maniacal about his laugh. And then, just as abruptly, he began to weep hysterically. A few minutes later he began to laugh again. And then, as before, he started to cry. For a full half hour the poor man alternated laughing and crying, laughing and crying. The rest of the group sat stunned, silent. After the man's fits of laughing and crying had run their course, the leader of the group reached over to touch him. Gently he prodded the minister to open up. "Maybe you want to share with us whatever triggered that?"

At this the minister began to talk. About his childhood. About growing up on a farm in Arkansas. About the fact that his father was a very macho man who loved to hunt and couldn't tolerate any sign of weakness in his son. And about that one awful time when his father, angered by his son's reticence about accompanying him on a rabbit-hunting expedition, had begun firing a rifle at his son's feet to taunt him. So terrified had the son become when his father had been firing those shots within inches of his feet, that he had begun to weep. And so relieved had he felt when he finally escaped from his father's clutches, running into the woods away from those hateful guns, that he then had laughed hysterically.

And so it was, listening to the most intimate revelations of these other clergymen, that I came to realize that everyone has his inadequacies and his dark secrets. What's more, it seemed, the most painful disabilities were not necessarily physical. During the six weeks, I had not opened up about my own dark secret. I was simply too uptight to reveal myself. But hearing the others talk, hearing their problems, I began to think, well, my situation isn't so bad after all. And then, just as the program was about to end—the dam broke—I finally managed to blurt it out.

I talked about my leg, my lifetime of shame, my feelings of inferiority. And the others, who had seen me respond with love and support when they disclosed their own painful secrets, now responded with love and support for me.

"Gee, Pesach," one clergyman told me, "you have such insight about other people. How could you possibly be worried about yourself? You are a compassionate person, and you have real feelings for others. You are special."

When I heard that, I felt like a thousand pounds had been lifted off my shoulders.

The second encounter, which occurred some years after my therapy sessions with the clergymen, was at a training group of the National Education Association in Bethel, Maine. This group was designed to deal with conflict management, and the participants included top managers from various fields—business executives, labor organizers, the head nurse in a national organization of nurses, and other important movers and shakers.

As a rabbi, I was particularly concerned about working with the boards of synagogues, with whom conflict is a natural, inevitable and ongoing by-product of making decisions and conducting business. That was why I joined the group.

As with the group therapy sessions involving the clergymen, it took a while for us to let down our defenses and get the show on the road. In the beginning, everybody had his guard up. Everybody was afraid he would be laughed at or looked down upon. Everybody had his vulnerable points. But after a while the members of the group got to know and trust each other. And slowly but surely that's when the masks began to crumble.

One of the participants was a tremendously successful railroad executive. He was a prim and proper man, a real Beau Brummell, always impeccably groomed and very controlled, and unfailingly dignified. He had a little mustache that he took great pains to shape and trim. Wearing silk ties and expensive English tweed jackets, he clearly prided himself on dressing to perfection. In fact, he did everything to perfection. You could see by his dress and his carriage that this was a man who was always in control. He was in control in his business, and he was in control in the group, where other people were beginning to bare their innermost secrets. No matter how intense or how shattering the revelations of the others, the railroad executive never lost his cool.

Then, one day, a very unusual thing happened. This dapper and controlled man, who had kept a stiff upper lip for so long, suddenly began to talk with great emotion, almost as if he were ready to cry. Proceeding slowly, pausing and sighing, barely restraining his tears, he said he had something he wanted to share with the rest of us.

"I had a dream," he began. "In my dream I was at a party. The party was held around a swimming pool, and lots of people were in the water, having a good time. It was a hot day, and everyone was splashing around, enjoying themselves. I walked out on the diving board. People started to shout to me, 'Come on in! John, join us! Join us!' At first I didn't want to. They kept urging. Then, finally, I said, 'All right.' They had convinced me.

"So I walked to the edge of the diving board, and I started to peel off my clothing. First I took off my shirt. Then I discovered that I was wearing another shirt under that first one. So I removed my undershirt too. But underneath my undershirt was *another* shirt. And underneath that one was another . . . and another . . . and another . . . and another. And that's when I became totally frantic."

The rest of the people in the group were quiet now.

In a voice cracking with emotion, the railroad executive continued. "I was afraid to go any further. Because maybe, just maybe, when I took off my last shirt, there would be nothing there. Nothing at all."

And then the railroad executive got to the real point of this dream: that inwardly he felt like a failure. Outwardly he had been a tremendous success. He was personable, gung-ho, fastidious, always in control. But inwardly he was convinced that there was nothing there, nothing at all, that he was a failure. He felt like a man who was living a lie. It was an incredibly moving confession.

When the railroad executive finished his story, he broke down and wept. The other members of the group immediately came to his aid. They told him that even though he had feelings of failure, in the group he had been a great success. Echoing the feelings of all of us, one member put it eloquently. "John, we've really been impressed by the way you related to the other people here. You've shown support and concern for us and our problems. This is your special-ness. By itself, success in the outer world means very little. It's the success that you feel inside that really counts."

All along, the railroad executive had viewed his life as a failure. But we had seen him in a very different light, when he was allowed to function in an environment that was not threatening. And to us he was a very good and very warm person.

The railroad executive's revelation had a tremendous impact on me. Once again it demonstrated that all of us, at one time or another, must wrestle with feelings of inferiority and inadequacy. But, for me, it also served as an object lesson . . . and helped me to take things one step further in my own self-awareness.

In the group, the railroad executive was unable to see himself as other people saw him. He did not see his potential or his specialness. It was only after that was pointed out to him that he began to understand his priorities were mixed up. He was concentrating on the wrong values in life— success, in worldly terms. True, success was important to his sense of self, but it was not sufficient. He needed more. By focusing exclusively on that success and the need to preserve it, he had lost sight of who he really was. What's worse, he had lost sight of who he had the potential to be.

The railroad executive's blinders made me think about my own situation, and I began to realize that I had done exactly the same thing. I had been so fixated on gymnastics and baseball and doing as well or better than the next guy that I was always focused on my sense of inferiority. I had spent many years wasting my energy, trying to gloss over or hide my feelings of inadequacy. I, too, had lost sight of who I was . . . and who I had the potential to be. Like the railroad executive, I needed someone else to tell me.

That affirmation came in the form of an unexpected letter that I received a few years later. The letter was written by Rabbi Alex Shapiro, a friend who had suffered a heart attack and had nearly died. In point of fact, I felt terribly guilty when I received his letter because I had been planning to write to him but had never gotten around to it. Yet, when I opened his letter, his message was not one of hurt over my inconsiderateness . . . but of gratitude.

"Pesach," he wrote, "you don't know what you've done for me! I am writing to thank you."

I was speechless. My God, I thought, what *have* I done? After my friend's heart attack, I had never gotten in touch with him, and the poor man had nearly died. I felt guilty and terrible.

But when I continued reading, the letter began to refer to something that had happened many, many years before, when my friend and I were counselors together at summer camp. "I remember you playing baseball and knocking homers," he wrote. "I remember you running around the bases. I had such tremendous admiration for you, Pesach, in overcoming your handicap. In the weeks after my heart attack, when it wasn't certain whether I would pull through or not, I thought a lot about your situation. And I must tell you that you were an inspiration to me.

"If Pesach could do it, I kept telling myself, then I can do it too."

Suddenly, as I read this letter, I felt myself jolted back through time. It was as if my rabbi friend had touched an invisible button and rewound the reel of my life. And I realized that during all those years when I was wrestling with those horrible feelings of inferiority, I was never aware of how *other* people were perceiving me. Like the railway executive, I never saw myself as I was. I never realized my potential. How much valuable time I had squandered. How much misunderstanding I had suffered.

Because of my preoccupation with my crippledness, I

wasn't aware of my power or my charisma. I wasn't aware of my specialness. My sense of inferiority had so much become my focus that I wasn't aware that I had entered another realm in the way I was meeting a life-challenging situation . . . and that, in that realm, I was performing superbly.

Looking back at my life, I now feel that my accident was one of the gifts—a bitter one, perhaps—that God gave me. Because of my struggles to overcome my physical handicap and to shed its heavy psychological baggage, I emerged a stronger, wiser, and more self-confident man. I had begun to find *my* meaning.

It took me many years to get in touch with this self-awareness, but it's what empowers me today. When I walk into a room at the hospital to visit a patient, I am able to say, well, here I am. But I don't have to put it into words. It's simply the way I am, my oneness as a person that I'm now aware of. It's the way I am able to bring with me my image of God, my specialness, that uniqueness which is in me, and which, after so many years of struggling, I can now understand.

As a result, I'm able to reach out to a person who is suffering and I'm able to do it without hiding behind a mask. Before I had that insight into who I really was, my uniqueness, I don't think I was truly able to reach out this way.

All of us must find that specialness. All of us must come to recognize that once we're gone, no one will ever replace us. That every moment is precious and cannot be repeated. If we can only bring out what we are without being afraid, if we can reach out, then we will all be open to creativity and creation, to nature, to the world, to its feeling, its excitement, its potentiality and possibility. Most important, we will be open to other people. We can even be open to those things which we ourselves must suffer.

CHAPTER

• 6 •

"Why Me?"—My Response to This Heartrending Question

"Whatever the universal nature assigns to any man at any time is for the good of that man at that time."

–MARCUS AURELIUS

"Rabbi, why me? What did I do to deserve such pain and misery?"

I know firsthand about that heartrending "Why me?" because it was a question that gave me a great deal of trouble as a teenager and young adult when I saw my friends whole and myself with a part missing. It took a long while before I came to realize that it was a pointless question, that the proper attitude was to accept what could not be changed and take responsibility to fulfill my own special potentialities in life. Rather than going down the blind alley of comparing myself to others, I learned to take stock of my own assets and to put them to the best possible use.

This knowledge put me in good stead the first time a patient grabbed my arm, looked at me with desperation, and pleaded, "Why me? Why does God punish me so?" It's a question I hear almost daily in different forms. Very often the patient will tell me tearfully what a good, honest, honorable life he has led, how he has tried to obey all the commandments, only to find himself cursed with a catastrophic illness.

That "Why me?" is sometimes shouted, "WHY ME?! Why did God do this to ME?" in such a way that I know the patient is beside himself with rage. Well, I never get into a theological discussion at that time because that's not what the patient is really seeking. Logic, at this point, will have little effect. It certainly will not be listened to. That comes later. First I have to deal with the emotions the patient is expressing.

Before I can speak to anyone who is hurting, I have to take care of the hurt. I know the difference between empathy and sympathy. Empathy, where you share in another person's emotions, allows you to feel with the other person but keep a distance where you can be of help. It's easy to express sympathy but it rarely does much good.

It was early in my rabbinical career that I grew to understand that sympathy alone was not the proper approach. I remember when frantic parents called to tell me their young son had committed suicide. I immediately rushed to their home. The house was bedlam. People were milling around, screaming. It was horrible. Now, if I had been only sympathetic, I would have joined that wild scene, tearing my hair out, not helping anyone. Of course I felt for them very deeply but, by keeping my objectivity, I was able to give some comfort to the bereaved family members.

"Why me?" is a cry of pain reflecting anger, grief, or even perplexity—and I must relate to the emotion the patient is expressing. If I know he's raging, I might respond, "This is terrifying. How can you take it?" or "If this happened to me, I'd be so angry I'd want to tear down the walls." I try to relate on whatever level he's feeling. Sometimes I will even admit my bewilderment and say, "I can't understand why God is doing this. We have questions to ask Him." But I've got to be right there with that patient.

I have found that it's important to listen intently with the heart as well as the mind. In his book *The Road Less Traveled*, the psychiatrist M. Scott Peck calls this technique "bracketing." That is, you have to eliminate all other thoughts and influences and put yourself in the patient's shoes.

If I am properly bracketed, the patient knows that I understand, care, and feel his pain. In accepting his emotions, I allow him to express feelings that he may not be able to voice to others, even to members of his family, because he believes they may not be able to take it. Being in control of his emotions rather than hiding them when everything seems out of control shores up the patient's dignity.

This is a relationship where I bring myself totally to this person in pain. And it doesn't mean "making nice." Doing so is, frankly, a lie. I know that many clergymen, feeling uncomfortable when they enter a patient's room, say "God will help you" and utter other bland words of encouragement. In doing so, they actually cut off this person. These well-wishers haven't related to or understood the depth of the patient's emotions. Or perhaps the load is just too much for them to handle. No, it is not appropriate to "make nice." You can't tell him, "Be strong," "Don't cry," or "Everything will be all right" when prospects are dim and the patient knows it. Instead, you've got to be right there with him, involved with his real feelings.

If you talk straight, a patient's natural response, even if he doesn't express it, is "Yes, this guy understands me." Once this happens, the patient feels free to pour out his bottled-up feelings. "This is hell . . . I'm so upset . . . I don't know how I can take it . . . Look at what I'm doing to my wife and family . . . I'm letting it all out and I can't help it . . . I'm so angry that this should happen to me."

When a patient's worst fears are confirmed, he frequently goes into shock, mercifully numbed into disbelief. Stages of denial, anger, and guilt may follow. An independent person all his life, he may now see himself as a burden on those close to him. If he feels there is no way out, that all escape hatches are blocked, depression may result. This can be a dangerous time, since thoughts of suicide may surface when a patient suffers overwhelming grief and sense of loss.

I am there with him as he goes through the valley of the shadow. When he finally comes to accept his circumstances, I challenge him to find a light, an exit, a path to follow.

If a patient tells me he doesn't believe in God, I don't try to convince him to become a believer. Following my own religious belief that I am God's messenger, I relate to him, to the battered soul within him, but I do not speak of it. I am there for him, to listen, to be with him in his pain and his anxiety and his depression.

When I am with that person, it's as if I am taking some of God's presence, that is, myself, my soul, and bringing it to him. By listening to him with such intensity, I elevate his self-worth and feed his dignity, or, as I would put it, his soul image. Even as I'm there for him and pray with him—or not pray with him—he feeds *my* soul because he gives me dignity in the way he responds. We sustain each other.

My greatest strength is gained through working with people who need my help. In my relationship with them, I find that I grow and I am nurtured.

Religious patients often find strength and comfort through their connection with their faith. Sometimes, however, they find it hard to reconcile their beliefs with the injustice of what has happened to them. One such patient was a thirty-five-year-old religious teacher who had studied for the rabbinate. A spot on his lungs had metastasized. Following an operation to determine the extent of the spread, doctors had told him that he had a sixty-five percent chance of recovery. That other thirty-five percent was a bitter blow to him. His misery was accentuated by the fact that his wife was to give birth soon and he might not be able to be there with her.

When I walked into his room, he had just received the news. He snapped at me. "What's happened to me? I can't believe it. Why is God punishing me? I don't know where I've sinned. I've never harmed anyone. I pray every day. I do good deeds. Why me?" He was so furious that he threatened to burn his prayer shawl and throw away his prayer books.

Jewish tradition allows and encourages the venting of anger. I didn't try to placate him or defend God or explain His actions. Instead, feeling the tone of his anger, I said, "This just doesn't make sense." I reached out and held his hand. By empathizing, by touching, by really listening and relating, I helped him through a bitter period.

Later, after many visits, he said to me, "Pesach, if my child is a son, I want to invite you to the *bris* (the circumcision ceremony). Maybe I do have a chance. I'm surely going to fight. Thanks for not asking me to deny my feelings. That I would not have been able to take."

I think that one thing that eventually has to come through in answer to the omnipresent question "Why me?" is the feeling and understanding that the circumstances of life may be beyond our control. But when it comes to what to do about the situation in which we find ourselves, we frequently have a good deal of control.

In explaining this to patients, I sometimes use the analogy of life being equivalent to a game of cards in which we have no say over the hand dealt us. We do, however, have control over how we play the hand. There's no point in blaming the dealer for a bad hand. The trick is to play it out with all the skill and determination at our command. And that is where I focus the patient's attention when I say, "Take responsibility."

Even in the gloomiest of times, when the situation seems most hopeless, a person can set an urgent, unfinished task for himself. He is responsible for bringing out the meaning of his life, based on his uniqueness and the singularity of each moment—a moment that can be lived only once and never retrieved. Everything really revolves around his making the most of his life; taking fate, the cards handed him, the circumstances over which he has no control, and heading for his destiny through meaningful choices, not so much by thinking but by actions. If he makes the most of every precious moment, he will have the incentive to carry on and add meaning to his life.

I don't have to speak to him about God. My presence bespeaks God. What I've said in effect, as God's messenger, is, "You are infinitely important to me. I love you. I feel for you." And then, after I've been with him through the depths of his despair—maybe even his bargaining with God—"If you do this, I will do that"—I'm ready to say to him, "Let's look at the next stage. Not the present one, where there seems no way out. But let's look at taking the responsibility for the time that you have."

If a patient is religious, I'll say "the precious gift that God has given you of time." If not religious, I'll simply say "the time that you have." I'll ask, "How can you fill this time with immediate action and with something else in the future, looking to the future to give you hope? There is always hope, even if you've been given a number of days or weeks or months. Doctors don't know anyhow for sure. They're not God. But what about some of the unfinished agenda you have? Remember, the masks are gone. Maybe it's saying 'I'm sorry' to someone. Maybe it's getting together with your children and opening up and talking honestly with them, telling your wife how much you love her, and showing her that."

I suppose it's a human failing that few ask "Why me?" when things are going smoothly, when one is blessed with health, good fortune, a happy, loving family, many friends. We seem to take these positive things for granted, as though we are entitled to them as a matter of course. That may seem to be true, but, unfortunately, all of us at one time or another must come face-to-face with adversity and loss. That is the human condition. To cope with these difficult conditions and transcend them, we must have a sense of perspective, to see the total pattern of our lives.

My dear friend, Rabbi Simcha Kling, has developed this sense of perspective. After surviving a quadruple bypass heart operation, he experienced sharp pains several weeks later. At that time his own surgeon was away on vacation, so he went to another doctor for treatment. However, the medication that this doctor prescribed caused heart failure and the rabbi stopped breathing. Miraculously, he was brought back from the dead. He later told me:

"Pesach, it was difficult for me and terrible for my family. But I have lived a full, creative, and mostly happy life. I cling to it with all my might. Yet, I am completely at peace. Each day I recite the traditional prayer: 'In your mercy and love and goodness, O Master of the Universe, you renew the works of creation.' I am ready to go whenever He calls . . . and with no regrets."

My friend's words stood me in good stead when, years later, I was faced with a terrible personal loss, the death of my first wife.

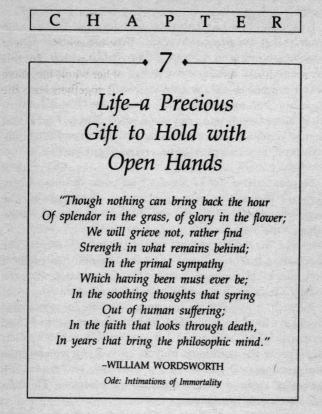

CHAPTER

• 7 •

Life–a Precious Gift to Hold with Open Hands

"Though nothing can bring back the hour
Of splendor in the grass, of glory in the flower;
We will grieve not, rather find
Strength in what remains behind;
In the primal sympathy
Which having been must ever be;
In the soothing thoughts that spring
Out of human suffering;
In the faith that looks through death,
In years that bring the philosophic mind."

–WILLIAM WORDSWORTH
Ode: Intimations of Immortality

I had felt for others in their grief and been there with them, but when the sharp tooth of grief bit into me I felt even more, and I understood.

When Muriel, my first wife, became ill with cancer fourteen years ago, and took a turn for the worse, we all knew that her days were numbered.

Suddenly time became very precious. All sham and reticence disappeared. What do you tell someone who is fatally ill and destined to die in the near future? Do you hide the facts? Some people do, when they believe the patient can't face it or the family is unwilling to deal with it. But this was not Muriel. As was characteristic of her whole life, there was no pretense, no cant. We faced it together, bore the heavy burden together, as one family—all was open. Every step of the terrible journey was revealed. She wanted it that way. The horror was faced head on—straight—realistically with fears, yes, but with firm courage and faith.

At the outset Muriel set down ground rules. She made it very clear that she would not trade pain for time. Every moment was precious because so little time was left. She wanted to savor each moment even if it were bought at the price of pain.

Since drugs would rob her of time and of her senses, she wouldn't take drugs—until the pain became unbearable. I remember how angry she was with the nurse who urged Valium upon her and which, in a weak moment, she took, and lost irreplaceable days. She couldn't forgive the nurse because she felt she had been robbed of priceless days and minutes.

Petty and useless talk disappeared. Each conversation became precious and fraught with meaning. Time—each moment, each hour, each day—became precious and was savored. Each sunrise was a glorious surprise. As the golden rays filtered through the kitchen window while we sat at the breakfast table, very much in love, the silence and the conversations pursued in depth were equally significant.

I learned so much from those last days we spent together. How priceless are those simple things—sunlight, a moment, a touch, family, friends, love. And how careless we are of our most valued treasures. We take them for granted, as if they are coming to us. As if we could hold on to them forever. That message of how priceless, how careless, runs through my mind each day when I counsel patients at the hospital.

After my wife's funeral I was approached by a member of my congregation, who said, "Rabbi, my son has heard. He's very upset at the injustice of your wife's death. He wants to know, 'How can you believe in God?' Would you please speak to him?" I called the son aside and we sat together in the hall. He listened intently as I quietly shared my thoughts with him. I said:

"Like yourself, some people ask why this tragedy happened to me. Why does God allow people who are so much worse, even evil, to go around hurting others and yet enjoying life while my wife, who was filled with the love of her people, so gracious and so wise, was taken away?"

The young man nodded agreement. "You know," I told him, "I never asked that question. That's a question a shattered heart asks. If you remember your Bible lessons, that's how Job felt when he raised his hand to the remote heaven and cried out: 'God hath torn me in His wrath and hated me. He hath gnashed upon me with His teeth; mine adversary sharpeneth His eye upon me.'

"I can understand how Job felt and sympathize with him, but these are not my questions. Actually, they are not good questions because they don't make the right assumptions about life."

"What, then, are the right assumptions?" the young man asked. Here is what I told him:

"Life isn't a matter of comparisons—my life in terms of someone else's life. Nor is it a series of measurements—the number of my years versus the number of somebody else's years. Nor is it a contrast in human values—my joys against another's—one way of death against another way of death. The judgment of God's justice and mercy is not in the mathematics of the years—nor in the sum of birthdays and anniversaries.

"Can we ask why wasn't Schubert's Unfinished Symphony drawn out into the longest symphony, or Lincoln's Gettysburg address, only two minutes, expanded into a longer oration? Each is a masterpiece, complete in itself.

"So is each life and so is each moment of our life. So that, if we died, the next moment of our life would be complete in itself. So was Muriel's life. So is each person's life—unique, complete in itself. So Muriel's life was not short because the life of another person may have had more years. Nor was her life less blessed because her passing was through the gates of pain.

"Where then is God? Where was He in Muriel's life? Where is He in anyone's life? These are the questions to ask: Was her life rich? How many lives did she touch? Was she a blessing to her family and friends and people with whom she had contact? Will she be missed—not only by her family but by those far from her? Did she take her joys humbly and gratefully? Did she meet her sorrows courageously? Was God present? Who can doubt it!"

When the young man left he thanked me profusely and said he now had a different perspective on what life could mean. He had learned something and, later, reflecting on Muriel's life and death, I learned something too.

She was grateful for joys and never took them for granted. Each day, to her very last, she said the blessings, "Thank you God for keeping me in life. Thank you God for another day." She saw life as a gift from God. A gift of which we are not deserving and which we could never repay, and which someday is returned (since it is not ultimately ours).

From my own experience, I learned the great truth of human existence: One must not hold life too precious; one must always be prepared to let it go. Muriel understood this and taught me. She held on to life, hands tight, because she treasured the moments as a gift—yet hands open to release because she knew that life, though precious, was a gift to be relinquished and returned. And God was here too—who could deny it?

Could I have held on to my beloved even one moment

longer—and put time into a deep freeze? Could I have enjoyed sunlight even one day longer with her, no matter how hard I tried? Could I have prevented night from falling? That moment had to pass. No power on earth could have retained it. Had I tried to hold back an irresistible force, it would have been a losing battle. At the end, I would still be left empty-handed and bitter about my loss.

Socrates put it very well when he said life is "a teacher in the art of relinquishing." Sooner or later we must bid farewell to the persons and things we love. Sometimes the separation is slow and peaceful and sometimes it is swift and violent. But the inevitable letting-go is something we must learn to accept and come to terms with.

As I see it, nothing can be more grotesque and more undignified than a futile attempt to retain what must be released. We must hold even our most precious possessions with open hands. That's a difficult concept. Many men and women cling so hard to a youthful image that they can't grow older gracefully. Sometimes marriages break up because of this frantic attempt by one or both partners to pursue and hold on to youth. And, of course, we all know parents who can't let go of their children, interfering with their lives, inflicting scars which years of therapy may later attempt to heal.

This is a hard lesson to learn. I think of those who have suffered the loss of a dear one or a loss of health who are never reconciled and who corrode their years and the lives of those around them with deep mourning, depression, and bitter complaints. Withdrawing from the sunlight into the dark shadows of despair, they forget that they are depriving loved ones who need them and that they have so much to add to life.

How do we let go of someone dear to us who has died? Following a mourning period, our focus must shift from a direct relationship to the departed to an identification with values we formerly shared. In that way, we free ourselves from the cold grip of the past to embrace warm and tender memories and action for the present.

A year following my wife's death, I delivered a sermon on the first day of Rosh Hashanah, the Jewish New Year. Drawing on teachings of the late Rabbi Milton Steinberg, here is part of what I said:

> We gather before the mystery of death to usher out a life through the instruments that tradition has given us. Even the most alienated often follow all the rituals in death. But how many of us take the time to celebrate life with all its love, and beauty and joy?
>
> I want to say to the husbands and wives who love one another, never accept your good fortune casually. In your breakneck pace through life, stop for a few moments and say a prayer in gratitude. Thank God for each day; don't take it for granted, while yet His sunlight shines on you.
>
> To parents, I want to remind you how precious is the gift of your children. Thank God each day for children; be aware of their little aggravations, but see the good and joy as well.
>
> I want to urge myself and all others to hold the world tightly yet lightly—to embrace life with all our hearts and all our souls and all our might. For it is a precious gift and sometimes we are careless, wantonly careless, with it.

CHAPTER

• 8 •

A Special Story About a Very Special Child

*"We have no power to fashion
our children as suits our fancy; As they
are given by God, so must
we have them and
love them."*

–JOHANN WOLFGANG VON GOETHE
Hermann and Dorothea

A world-famous scientist is frequently seen on one side of
the human scale and a retarded child on the other. Yet, as we
are told in Genesis, God made man by breathing into him
"the breath of life," and there is a part of the divine in each of
us. If a person can find his song or his task—it doesn't matter
what it is as long as it is his own—then his life can have
meaning. In that context I would like to relate my experiences with a very special child and his very special family.

Jesse's parents, who were members of my congregation, came to me about two years before their son's thirteenth birthday and told me they wanted him to be "bar-mitzvahed," for him to experience the religious service through which a Jewish boy crosses the threshold into young manhood.

I thought to myself, "How is that possible?" Jesse was severely retarded and had a speech impediment. Despite that, however, he was given enormous love and affection by his parents and family. His learning ability was close to zero. But he was a very loving and lovable child and his very devoted parents felt strongly that he should have the opportunity. So we decided to give it a try.

We were fortunate that we had a teacher in our religious school who was having phenomenal success in teaching children with learning disabilities. Working with Jesse, she developed many new approaches, using movements, sounds, and various colored balls to identify each letter in the Hebrew alphabet. After countless hours of painstaking work with complete concentration and devotion, she taught Jesse the first two blessings for the reading of the Torah, the sacred scroll.

The bar-mitzvah day arrived. Jesse's parents had invited many people from the community and beyond to the synagogue, including some who also had mentally disabled children. The place was packed. Everyone knew Jesse and was on edge, silently rooting for him.

There was a hush when Jesse rose to recite his blessings. It took a great deal of time for him to laboriously sound out each letter: "B-a-a-a-a, r-o-o-o-o . . . u-u-u-u . . . ch," and so on. Miraculously, he was able to complete his chore. What ordinarily takes a minute to say took him fifteen minutes. And everyone was hanging on to each letter as he pronounced it.

How tenaciously he struggled and how overjoyed he was when he successfully completed his recitation. His face lit up, beaming with a broad smile. Everyone in the congregation was also smiling, but there was many a surreptitious tear too.

In my sermon I tried to speak words appropriate to the occasion. I chose the story *The Missing Piece*, by Shel Silverstein, a wonderful children's book which had had an enormous impact on me because of its validity for my own circumstances.

As I recall it, this is a story about a big wheel, a fabulous wheel, the fastest wheel of all. It outraced every other wheel and took a great deal of joy and pleasure out of doing that. One day it was wheeling along, having the greatest time, when a terrible thing happened. It hit a bump and lost a piece of itself.

Now, with a chunk missing, the wheel went clunk, clunk, clunking along and couldn't keep up with the other wheels. It was very sad. Life had lost all meaning. Very distressed, it started journeying great distances to search for its missing piece.

As the wheel traveled, clumping along, it grew tired and lay down on a field of grass. For the first time, it felt the warm and friendly earth underneath it. And it looked straight up for the first time and saw the white clouds against the deep blue sky and heard the birds sing beautiful songs. It had time to speak to the birds, and to children, and to grown-ups too. "Oh, this is wonderful," the broken wheel said. "I never had these kinds of experiences before."

Well, years passed. Finally the wheel found its missing piece in a far-off land. Overjoyed, it made itself whole again and whirled around saying, "Oh, great." This went on for several weeks, until the wheel realized that something was missing in its life. "I wasn't listening to the birds. Didn't take time to look at the sky. Didn't watch any butterflies. Didn't feel how wonderful it was to lie back tired on the earth and rise refreshed."

I bet you can guess what that wheel did. It yanked out the

recently attached piece and threw it away. That wheel had learned a most important lesson—that it was actually more whole when a part of it was missing.

Closing my sermon, I said, "We must all learn to look past visible disabilities to discover and appreciate the essential divine spark within every human being. Jesse has that special faculty of giving love. Most of us have to look for our meaning in life, and struggle to find it. Jesse found it from his very birth. He just gives all that love and his parents have given him an environment where they give him love, too—so that he has grown and they have grown."

Following that bar mitzvah, Jesse had various illnesses, was hospitalized often, but pulled through each time. He required a great deal of attention, just like a frail flower or a plant, more so than an ordinary child. Finally, he could no longer continue and he passed away, leaving a great gap in the family and heavy grief.

If I had a message for parents of special children, it would be to recall the words of the boxer Muhammad Ali, who boasted, "I am the greatest." He said it about himself and he really meant it.

Well, each one of us can say about ourselves, "I am the greatest," because of the great potential within ourselves. Each one of us is unique, special, and will never be here again. We have to discover for ourselves that uniqueness and specialness through what we do, our daily tasks and how we perform them, how we take responsibility for our lives.

Jesse had his specialness. He expressed his genius in giving love. He loved the way a child does, without protective armor, for all of his life, and I think most special children have that quality about them. Maybe intellectually they do not measure up, but when it comes to love, what I call the spiritual part, they have far more than their normal share. Especially when they are nurtured by a family, they grow bright and beautiful like a flower.

Many mothers and fathers of children with learning or

other disabilities frequently blame themselves for the child's handicap and suffer needless feelings of shame and guilt. Allowed free rein, these feelings play havoc with a family and can hurt the personality development of the disabled child, making him either overdependent or even hostile. On the other hand, loving parents, unburdened by misplaced personal emotional distress, who accept the child as he is in this most difficult situation, will help him achieve to the best of his abilities.

If parents with special children give of themselves, even though it demands so much of their time and energy and the family pulls together, the rewards can be beyond measure. With the love shown and expressed through the child, the family grows. The family strengthens its bonds and becomes more compassionate. In a sense the family finds its meaning in tending to such a special child.

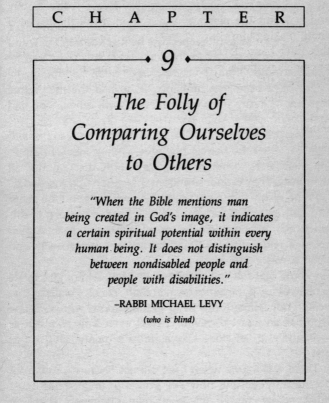

CHAPTER

• 9 •

The Folly of Comparing Ourselves to Others

"When the Bible mentions man being created in God's image, it indicates a certain spiritual potential within every human being. It does not distinguish between nondisabled people and people with disabilities."

–RABBI MICHAEL LEVY

(who is blind)

A long time ago I learned the hard way about the difference between asset values, where you are aware of your own specialness, and comparative values, where you constantly compare yourself to others.

In the previous chapter I called Jesse a genius in love and compassion. He was completely open and unprotected because, unlike most of us, he did not wear a mask and keep his guard up. We are frequently afraid to show our feelings for many reasons. Perhaps we're concerned that someone may laugh at us. Or maybe we believe in hiding our feelings so that we never reveal weaknesses.

Jesse loved everyone. From the asset value, he didn't have to struggle for recognition because he just knew it, the way a flower gives its beauty for beauty's sake. It is there and he was there too. From the comparative value standpoint, he might have been very unhappy if he had the intellectual capacity or desire to compare himself with others who had more brain power than he.

Many people with physical handicaps, who are crippled, have accepted the perfect physique as their ideal. Comparing themselves to others, they are bitterly disappointed all their lives. They cannot surmount that vision or transcend it.

I find it truly sad to see the loss experienced and the anger and guilt felt by those who are crippled and trapped in this emotional prison. I'm distressed because, despite their courage and resilience, they are on the wrong track, and what a waste that is.

I know that full well from my own life. Although I made captain of my gymnastics team in high school, I realized that I could not compete effectively in most sports with someone who has an intact physique. I can't even walk as much as someone else, let alone hike as far. I certainly can't run as fast.

There was a time when I felt inferior because I could not do these things. But now I've grown to understand that I must compare myself only to my own uniqueness, that I am a whole person, not different from others, because everyone, in a sense, has a part missing. No one is perfect. And until I learned the basic truth of my own uniqueness and concentrated on it, I suffered a lot of unnecessary sorrow and anger and guilt.

That's a hard lesson to learn. I recall reading that the American athletes were bitterly disappointed when so few fans showed up for the U.S. Olympics for the Disabled.

Similarly, the Israeli athletes who won a world championship for the disabled were angry and frustrated that films of their games were not shown on Israeli television. In both cases, the athletes made the mistake of comparing themselves to the athletes in the regular Olympics.

All of us are crippled in the sense that we have unresolved internal conflicts that prevent us from functioning at our top levels. And we all know how big left field is—that's the area from which so many unexpected problems hit us. Things are always happening that put a damper on how we think, feel, and act. Even the most outwardly successful people in our society—writers, composers, scientists, captains of industry—experience soul-searching periods when they question their accomplishments, their self-worth, and consider themselves failures and inferior to others.

The "cripple" factor is most obvious in people with physical handicaps, but no one is immune to feeling inferior. Earlier I wrote about the eminently successful railway executive who felt that he was a zero, that he hadn't accomplished anything. And in my group therapy with the ministers I covered up the dark secret of my own handicap. You can imagine my amazement when I learned that everyone there had his own secret, a lifetime of heavy baggage that really weighed him down. That certainly made it easier for me to lighten my own burden.

The lesson hit home that a person's ultimate adjustment to a disability is closely related to his attitudes and values. I don't want to deny the fact that a disabled person does face many difficulties because of physical limitations and the real factors of environment. However, the disability is not as others see it as much as it is the disabled person's own perception.

If a person becomes crippled, his total functioning, his feelings of dignity and self-worth, are affected. His adjustment depends on the self-image he held before his accident or illness about the "whole body"—the perfect physique. If he insists on comparing himself to the intact person, he will always be imperfect in comparison and feel inferior, half a person. This is impoverished soil in which feelings of shame, guilt, embarrassment, and worthlessness take root.

In his view, his social status is low and he may feel degraded because of his inferiority. His impotence is overwhelming. People regard him as a burden and feel that he cannot contribute his fair share. Girls won't want to go out with him. They will be repulsed by the sight of him. Now, that's how the disabled person often thinks people see him. And these feelings may be real or imagined.

Suppose you're a crippled person and that others really do have negative feelings about you. You can always find someone who will pity you or put you down as part of a minority or disadvantaged group. If you allow yourself to accept these outside valuations of yourself, you will doubt your own self-worth and this distorted viewpoint becomes a self-fulfilling prophecy.

As a result, you may become completely unaware of or won't even trust the fact that many people view you with the highest regard. They may see you as a brave and honorable person who has faced difficult circumstances, surmounted his handicap, and come out a beautiful human being. They may deeply admire you because, in a sense, they themselves are struggling with the same issues of self-worth that you are. And you may give them courage.

If you're disabled, there should come a time when you become cognizant of your strengths, drop any feelings of worthlessness, and say to yourself, "I am a whole person despite my handicap." Take onto yourself the viewpoints of those who look up to you. The most successful people are those in every walk of life who know who they are, accept who they are, and live who they are.

If a handicapped person idealizes the "normal" standards, he relegates himself to a permanent inferior position. To forget and conceal his disability, he must act as if he were not

different from others. Such unrealistic behavior only reinforces feelings of guilt and inferiority.

The cycle spirals. Attempting to escape inferior feelings,
such a person competes as if he had no handicap, inevitably
fails, and becomes increasingly resentful of an unjust world.
The harder he struggles, the more he is rejected by the
"normal" society. He remains the marginal man, belonging
to neither one group nor the other. Until he accepts himself
as he is, he will not achieve identity integration.

In the real world, a person who becomes seriously ill or
physically disabled is forced to be somewhat dependent,
even if only temporarily. However, if he is seriously crippled,
he must learn to accept a degree of lifelong dependency in
some respects.

That's not an easy thing to do. Some people often deny
their need for help in order to maintain their precious image
of independence. If a person hides his dependency needs
and pushes himself to the limits of his ability and endurance,
he may progress outwardly but pay a high price in malad-
justment.

Fortunately, there are powerful forces pushing the disabled person to take an active part in making the appropriate
adjustment. Reality factors of ongoing life, work, community, family, and recreation drive him to accept his disability
and accept himself as he is. The strain of hiding may exact
too high and painful a cost of psychic energy.

I believe motivation is the key factor in overcoming a
handicap. In my experience, patients who are strongly
motivated to get better frequently improve remarkably
despite severe physical handicaps, whereas mildly disabled
patients who consider themselves as hopeless invalids may
remain that way for the rest of their lives.

If a person attempts to "compensate" for his loss by
emphasizing some other attributes, he frequently finds
himself on a dead-end road. Seen in the perspective of asset
values, a disabled person has nothing to compensate or

make up for. He need have no shame or guilt. However, value changes are sometimes appropriate. A person who turns to painting because of a heart condition may find that art has a significant value, too—and a person's worth is not connected with his physique.

I know from my own experience that a disabled person is on the rewarding road to self-fulfillment when he accepts his handicap and no longer compares himself to the non-injured as the wished-for ideal. Once you realize that you have a self-image that is dragging you down, you can discard that excess baggage, concentrate on your positive and creative aspects, and express your specialness. If you recognize your own asset values, you won't seek artificial means, such as drugs, to sustain you. Just being yourself and opening yourself to the wonders and opportunities of this life will be fulfilling.

That's when you move out of the suffocating perspective, narrow and bleak, that all is lost, nothing is left, to the fresh air and wider perspective that life holds many possibilities and surprises. Your loss then becomes a dab of paint on a broad canvas of colors, varied and rich, that depict a person's whole life.

Every human being has certain aspects of his life that touch other human beings. We want to feel that we are worthwhile, that we do count, that we have dignity and a sense of responsibility. We are all subject to events and environments that we didn't create. And everything depends on how we respond to them, how we interpret them, and whether we are submerged by them or surmount them. If we can go beyond them, we can use the most difficult circumstances as rungs on a ladder, in a sense, heavenward.

Much of the time we wear masks and, very often, there's deep hurt under a smiling mask. Perhaps we feel that we have behaved badly, that people dislike us, that things are out of control, that we have failed. All this goes back to the patient in the hospital. Because suddenly that person feels that he is deprived, "crippled," unable to cope. If he can look within himself and take responsibility for the impediment he faces and use his losses constructively, it makes all the difference in the world.

This brings to mind the story of a particular patient I will never forget. He was a very old man who was recuperating from a colostomy, a most debilitating operation. When I entered his hospital room, he looked up at me and said, "Rabbi, please don't sympathize with me. I'm really happy."

Taken aback, I asked him, "What do you mean?"

"Well," he said, "I'm alive. If I hadn't gone through this and it hadn't been discovered, I would have had, the doctor said, one more year to live, in deep pain. I'm really very happy about it. The trouble is that I didn't pay for this."

I didn't understand his reference to payment and asked him what he meant. Here's what he told me:

"You see, when I go out to buy a car, I might spend fifteen, twenty thousand, or even more. That could be a lot of money for me, and you can be darn sure that I'm going to polish that car, keep its motor up to par. It's an investment and I had to work to get it.

"Health, however, is given us for free. We don't pay for it, so we take this most precious possession for granted. It's only when it's removed that we realize how fortunate we were and would give all our savings just to have enough health to live one year, two years, five years, ten years without pain. I now know how valuable it is.

"And after what I've been through I really appreciate my family and my friends for their support and love. Every day I get up will be a new day for me. How wonderful! There are so many things I have to do before I kick the traces. I'm going to get well and I'm going to use my days as I've never done before."

Now, this man was in his eighties. Perhaps he had not lived, truly, in the sense of being alive to all that was around him, and the treasures that were within his grasp. But I could be certain that he was going to live every day left to him in the greatest depth. And I think that is what life is all about.

A wonderful example of a man who was able to transcend his disability, express his uniqueness, and find his meaning is my good friend Art Nierenburg, who had polio and became a wheelchair-bound paraplegic. Instead of succumbing to his disability, he did wonders from a wheelchair. He created a factory, called it Abilities Unlimited, and brought together the most handicapped people.

I remember going through his plant, which produced delicate and intricate electronics components that competed in the marketplace. The people on the assembly line were severely disabled but all were well trained. I recall one man whose body was just a trunk with no arms and no legs and who was working with his mouth.

Because of the extraordinary job that Nierenburg had done, executives of top corporations invited him to tell them how to get a factory work corps to function at its highest potential. But although he was successful, Art felt dissatisfied. He told me that he was always angry because he had to constantly prove himself and show others that he was better than they were. That drained him tremendously. He was wasting his energies.

One day he came to the realization that he had to accept himself as he was, that he could express his own uniqueness and find his meaning without comparing himself to anybody else. He left the factory to become a worldwide lecturer. Wherever he goes he speaks to disabled people who doubt their value to society or themselves, and he gives them the courage to create and to do.

It all comes down to the question of finding meaning in our lives. Jung has said every one of his patients who were over thirty-five had what were, in a broad sense, religious problems, because they were railing at their boredom and the meaningless of their lives. People under pressure, as in a serious hospital situation, suddenly come face-to-face with the question of their life's meaning.

We would all do well to focus on this question before we become ill. Let's face it. Meaning is crucial because we are all terminal. We're not aware of the ticking away of time until we reach a certain age. Then we realize that life has an end. That focuses us on what to do with the remaining time, since we cannot recover the past.

How can we make the most of this precious gift of life that we have? Let's not wait for a time when we retire, relocate, and perhaps find disappointment. Each day has to be a new beginning. Each day that we awake has to have its meaning. Each day is a canvas upon which we paint the picture of our lives. So the question poses itself, "What are we going to do with the time we have to make the most of this magnificent and sometimes terrible world in which we live?"

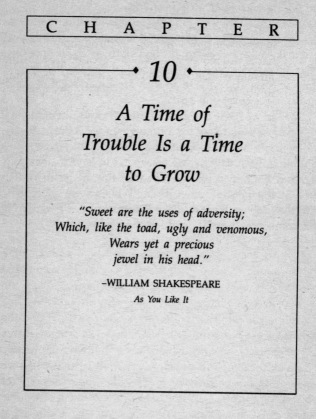

CHAPTER

• 10 •

A Time of Trouble Is a Time to Grow

"Sweet are the uses of adversity;
Which, like the toad, ugly and venomous,
Wears yet a precious
jewel in his head."

–WILLIAM SHAKESPEARE
As You Like It

Adversity can be a path of growth for all of us, regardless of handicap, physical or otherwise. That's because life, in a sense, can be compared to the making of fine china: Like clay, it must be exposed to searing flame before it emerges shaped and beautiful.

Before Franklin D. Roosevelt was afflicted with polio, he gave little evidence of greatness or even of sympathy for the ill and underprivileged. Viewed from the perspective of history, his affliction, however painful for him, may seem a small price to pay for producing a dedicated leader in the hour of world crisis.

We all suffer losses of varying degree throughout life. Like the tree that is pruned and bursts with greater growth, the human soul may be damaged and bruised in life, providing an opportunity for the individual to get in touch with the depths of God's divinity in the universe, which gives hope and courage in return.

To illustrate this truth, I sometimes tell patients the parable about the two woodchoppers who had taken down a tree that was over one hundred years old. Looking at the growth rings to determine the tree's age, the younger man noticed that there were five very narrow rings. He concluded that there had been a five-year drought, during which the tree had shown very little growth.

However, the other lumberman, a wise, older man with a philosophical bent, had a different viewpoint. He contended that the dry years actually were the most significant in the tree's history. His reason: Because of the drought, the tree had to force its roots down farther to get the water and the minerals it needed. With a strengthened root system, it was able to grow faster and taller when conditions improved.

As with the tree, human beings experience times when we reach obstacles that seem to exclude the possibility of progressing further. It is precisely at these times of trouble that we must grow inwardly. If we do, we will be amazed at how we can expand our horizons when the right conditions prevail again.

Ecclesiastes holds that it is better to go to a House of Mourning than to a House of Rejoicing, for in the House of Mourning one is able to learn so much more. In all history, there was no greater House of Mourning than in the concentration camps of Nazi Germany during the Holocaust of World War II. Yet, even in those cauldrons of human misery, it was possible for some fortunate few to find hope and, yes, growth.

One of the seminal thinkers for me is a man named Viktor Frankl. A Jewish psychiatrist, he was imprisoned in a Nazi concentration camp. From that bleak and deadly experience, he distilled a book, *From Death Camp to Existentialism*, which he later titled *Man's Search for Meaning*.

In the concentration camp, Frankl soon became a zero like everybody else, just a faceless number. As he describes it, he became like a dog, scrounging for food in his struggle to hang on to life. All he thought about was a crust of bread for which he might be prepared to kill. He had lost all semblance of humanity.

One day he had an insight. He stopped short and said to himself, "I'm a psychiatrist and this is an extraordinary laboratory of human relations under miserable conditions. Here I can learn so much about how human beings relate to one another under periods of terrible stress and use that knowledge someday working with my patients."

Frankl noticed that some people survived and others didn't. And it wasn't a result of their physical strength. Strong young men were dying and some feeble old women were carrying on. "Why is this happening," he wondered. "What makes the weaker person stronger? What keeps him going?"

Trying to solve that problem, he began to carefully observe his fellow prisoners and to take notes. He thought to himself, "Someday I'm going to lecture to learned societies about the unique insights I'm gaining here." From that time on, his prison life was transformed. He forgot about bread, forgot about water, and was excited each day. He reports that he couldn't wait for the next day even though it would bring new terror and torment.

From his observations, Frankl came to the realization that the most important life force for man is not the drive for sex, as Freud saw it, or the drive for power that Adler spoke about, but the search for meaning. He found a profound truth, in Nietzsche's words: "If you have a *why* to live for, you can bear with any *how*."

It dawned upon him that every human being has to have a task. If he can find his song, or his task—it doesn't matter what it is but it has to be his own—he can keep his dignity with a sense of hope and can transcend even the most desperate circumstances.

Once he had found his own task, Frankl had renewed zeal and zest for life. Searching out others with hope, he saw an old woman who was knitting socks for her grandchildren—and surviving. Another inmate, a young intellectual, had dreamed he would be liberated by Christmas and was living for that day. The closer he came to Christmas, the more agitated he became. When the longed-for day passed, all hope was lost. He had nothing to live for and died soon after. Frankl writes:

> Those who know how close the connection is between the state of mind of man—his courage and hope or lack of them—and the state of immunity of his body will understand that the sudden loss of hope and courage can have a deadly effect. The ultimate cause of my friend's death was that the expected liberation didn't come and he was severely disappointed. This suddenly lowered his body's resistance against the latent typhus infection. His faith in the future and his will to live had become paralyzed and his body fell victim to illness.

The intellectual died when his window of hope slammed shut, but the little old lady survived because she still hoped to see her grandchildren. It's not very different in my hospital. A patient with a strong life-goal sometimes can prolong his life by three, six, or nine months or even longer because he wants, say, to be present at the marriage of his son or daughter. Often he makes it because his mind sends a message to his body which says, "Hey, hold up, I'm going to be there and you're going to let me be there."

Sending messages to your body really works. Suppose you're being threatened by a mugger. What happens? Either you freeze or your adrenaline begins to flow and you fight back or run. A message has been delivered: Danger! As I look at it, the chemist within you, which is God-given, provides the wherewithal you need for survival. In a hospital setting, the chemicals provided may be self-generated substances which combat disease elements and thus provide healing power.

The human mind does more than just play tricks on us from time to time. It plays an important part in prolonging or shortening life. I recall reading in medical literature about the case of a man suffering from Hodgkin's disease, enduring swelling, pain, and great discomfort. He traveled a great distance to a particular hospital that had permission for experimental use of a new drug. He received an injection and, miraculously, the swelling subsided, the pain diminished, and he went home, cured for a while.

Four months later, the same dire symptoms came back and he returned to the hospital. This time the hospital was out of the drug but didn't tell him. Instead, they gave him a placebo, an innocuous injection of sugar and water that resembled the original drug. Again, the swelling went down, the pain eased, and he went home.

Another four months passed and again the disease acted up. The hospital now had the drug available for use. When the patient arrived at the hospital, he said, "I know that a Congressional committee has investigated the drug and found that it's completely useless against Hodgkin's disease. But I came back anyway because I'm desperate."

He received the injection, went home, and died soon thereafter. He had lost hope completely and his body succumbed. Yes, miracles sometimes happen when there is even a little gateway of hope.

But hope alone frequently is not enough. People also need a *why*, a direction for their lives to strengthen them to endure the sometimes terrible *how* of their existence. This need is not necessarily focused upon someone with no way out in a death camp. Philosophers point to modern man, who is in deep trouble, with a sense of aimlessness, boredom, and with no awareness of meaning to his life. Finding your task or, as I like to put it, finding the image of God within you, can make all the difference in the world in what you get out of life.

This is borne out in dramatic fashion in a case history Viktor Frankl relates about a woman patient who had a miserable life. She had had two children. Her elder son, brilliant and handsome, the apple of her eye, was killed in an accident. Her younger son was born a quadriplegic, paralyzed from the neck down. She tended to this son to the best of her ability but her heart was broken by the calamity that had befallen her.

Paraphrasing Frankl, here is how the situation unfolded. One day she told her son, "This is no life for you and this is no life for me. I'll give you poison and I'll take poison and we won't have to struggle anymore."

Her son refused to go along, telling her, "I want to live. You have no right to take my life away from me. And you don't have the right to take your own life." And so there she stayed, left with no way out, continuing to devote herself day and night to her son's welfare.

When she came to Frankl's office she was depressed and distraught. During a group therapy session in which she participated, Frankl asked another member to play-act, to pretend that she was an eighty-five-year-old woman, a very wealthy socialite with no children but many material possessions. "You're on your deathbed," he told her, "and you're looking back at your life. What do you see?"

The woman thought for a while and then responded: "Well, I had everything. Life was a bowl of cherries. I traveled widely, had many lovers. I had no children. When I look back, I see nothing of value."

Then Frankl turned to the troubled woman and said, "Now you are eighty-five years of age, on your deathbed, and you're looking back at your own life. What do you see?"

She began to talk, telling about her tragedies and said, "You know, when I look back, I think mostly of my son, whom I love very much and who shows me much love. I've devoted my whole life to him and it's been a hard but wonderful life. I've kept him alive and he's made something valuable of his life too." She was transfixed and began to cry. Looking back, she knew that she had become aware of her task, her self-worth, and her purpose.

Viktor Frankl notes that she left the group and took up her life with a new zest and appreciation. She had found her "why" and could take any "how." I would say that she had found her own song.

Like Frankl, I find myself in a hospital trying to help patients look back into their lives to learn what gave them their greatest strength in meeting problems and to encourage them to draw upon these same resources in their present difficulties. After a patient has received the bad news and I've been with him as he worked out his grief, I confront him by telling him that his life has a past, a present, and a future—and he has a choice about how to deal with his circumstances.

In essence, I tell him that if he puts his past into his present, his past becomes his present and he is encapsulated within the past. Closing off all exits, he is then unable to cope with his present reality. On the other hand, if he puts his future into his present—namely all the worries and the angers and the fears that are buffeting him about and giving him no rest—then that becomes his present and he has no present whatsoever.

Instead of becoming a prisoner of his past or allowing himself to be shackled by the fears for his future, he has the ability to gain a new perspective on his life. If he focuses on the fact that every moment is a gift to be cherished and lived, this may provide a unique opportunity to experience life in its greatest depth. Now is the time, I tell him, to take responsibility for his life, to straighten out his priorities and not sap his strength by dwelling on the memories of his past or the uncertainties of his future. Most important, he has to set specific tasks and goals for himself and keep his eye on that ever-present window of hope.

The truth of this was reinforced for me by three disparate events that happened at around the same time—the freeing of Natan Sharansky, the Jewish dissident in the Soviet Union; the death of former Senator Jacob Javits; and the suicide of Donald Manes, the disgraced former president of the borough of Queens in New York City.

Sharansky had been behind iron bars for years. Punished by extended solitary confinement to break his spirit, he seemed to have had little hope. Javits was imprisoned by his own body and couldn't speak or keep his head up without the supportive collar he wore. Manes, however, was healthy, had all his faculties, but was imprisoned from within. He had been so shamed by his actions, was so devoid of hope for the future, that he committed suicide.

What gave Sharansky strength was his connection to his people, to his culture, and to the worldwide messages of encouragement he received. That gave him dignity. Because he felt he was not alone and was in control of his destiny despite his confinement, he always had a window of hope.

Javits also never gave up. He achieved his greatest status after being afflicted by a paralyzing illness sometimes called Lou Gehrig's disease. Speaking out to provide inspiration to others with incurable ailments, Javits said: "We are all terminal—we all die sometime—so why should a terminal illness be different from terminal life? The most positive therapy is to perpetuate the life force, and whether the patient is a mechanic or a U.S. Senator, he or she has a motivation which must prevail over the illness." At Javits's funeral, Senator Alan K. Simpson of Wyoming said, "The illness that had crippled him could have imprisoned a lesser man but, in his case, the spirit soared."

The lessons from the fates of these three very different men apply to all of us. We all have moments of despair. We all face the problems of illness, aging, the death of close ones, loneliness. Life is paved with pitfalls—losing a job, losing health, failing a test, feeling that we have failed ourselves, our parents, our spouses.

To transcend our losses, we must be sustained by the knowledge and faith that if we search hard enough and long enough, we can find and keep open that essential window of hope. Hardship and adversity, properly utilized, can provide the surest way to revitalize and remotivate ourselves. A time of trouble is truly a time to grow.

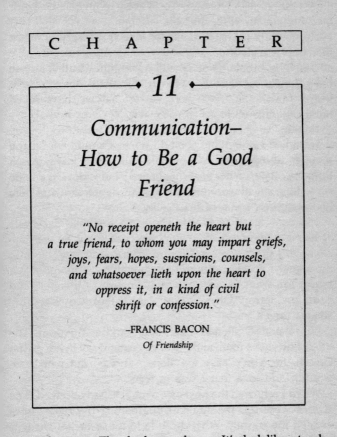

Communication– How to Be a Good Friend

"No receipt openeth the heart but a true friend, to whom you may impart griefs, joys, fears, hopes, suspicions, counsels, and whatsoever lieth upon the heart to oppress it, in a kind of civil shrift or confession."

–FRANCIS BACON
Of Friendship

I enter the room. The shades are drawn. It's dark like a tomb.

The patient, a thirty-year-old man named Jules, has lost a leg in a motorcycle accident. When I first met him a year ago he was wearing a Rolling Stones T-shirt, a captain's hat parked jauntily on his head, his red hair knotted in the back. Chipper. Self-confident. "Doctors give me little hope," he told me. "I'll fight it." And he did, returning to the hospital from time to time.

Now he's back for another chemo treatment. Gradually fading, he has little strength left. We had become very friendly in my previous visits. He always called me Pesach, my first name, never Rabbi.

This time I open the door and a blinding light streams in from the corridor behind me. An anguished cry greets me from the dull gray mass lying in bed. "Pesach, get out of here! I don't want to see you! Pesach, leave me now. Leave me alone."

What can I say? What should I do? For a moment I stand there in stunned silence, hesitate, turn, and leave. Later, thinking about what had happened, I decide I must do something drastic to break through his depression and help him recapture some of his vitality.

The next day I returned. The same tomblike darkness, same mass, inert in bed. When Jules cries out as he sees me, "Pesach, I don't want to see you, please leave me," I enter the room. I speak out with determination. "This room is a tomb. You want to die, don't you? Enough of this hell, and pain, and terror? Okay. If you want it that way. Keep the shades down."

No response. Silence. I exit and stand at the door. The nurse enters the room and I hear the patient say to her, "That Pesach, he won't leave me alone." It was said with such warmth and love that I was in tears.

When I returned the next day, a miracle had occurred. The shades were up, the sunlight brightening the room. Jules greeted me warmly. What did I do to cause such a change? Well, I told him, in effect, "I'm here. You're not alone. I care for you. I love you. I won't abandon you." I didn't say these words, which might have embarrassed him, but they were implicit.

"Jules, you have some living to do yet," I told him. "What are you going to do with the gift of time that God has given you?"

No longer feeling desperately alone, he had turned

around to life and away from death, facing the tasks he had yet to do.

When I enter a patient's room, I frequently feel inadequate, sad, angry, deeply puzzled. What can I say to this patient? What can I offer? How can I help? I've discovered that to get into the real world of the patient, I first must open a channel of effective communication.

Getting a patient to talk freely, openly, and honestly is possibly the most difficult task of all. He and I have to be on the same wave length. In this regard, I sometimes tell a humorous story of a woman who came to an attorney for help in obtaining a divorce from her husband.

"Do you have grounds?" the attorney asked.

"Oh, yes, we have half an acre."

The lawyer paused, then continued. "Do you have a grudge?"

The woman responded, "Oh, no, we have a carport."

In desperation, the lawyer plunged ahead, asking, "Does he beat you up?"

She enthusiastically responded, "Oh, no, I get up earlier than he does."

Unable to contain himself any longer, the exasperated attorney shouted, "Madam, exactly why do you want a divorce?"

Innocently she replied, "Because it's impossible to communicate with him."

Some years ago I had a communications problem of another sort when I was myself a patient in a hospital. I had had surgery, was in pain, and a nurse was giving me a hard time. Since I couldn't get off the bed, I had to call her for a drink, a urinal, or whatever. It took an exasperatingly long time for her to respond. When she did arrive, she'd practically throw the objects at me in a very angry manner. Trying to establish a relationship, I started to say, "You must be very busy," but she scooted out before I got the words out.

When I was able to get into a wheelchair, I rolled over to the nurse's station, and there she was. I was going to say something to her, but another patient beat me to it. He had probably had an experience similar to mine and he lambasted that nurse. "You aren't worthy of being a nurse!" he shouted. "You should be a chambermaid. You're a complete failure. You don't have the faintest notion of what being a nurse means."

The nurse responded with righteous indignation. "What gives you the right to talk to me like that?" she exploded. "I'm a trained nurse with ten years of experience." The patient was not impressed. "You're a nothing," he said, and stalked away. At this, the nurse broke into tears and ran down the corridor.

The next time she came to my bed, I said to her, "I was really upset about how that patient spoke to you. But you know, you've also caused me some distress." And I told her how I felt about the way she responded to my needs. I was careful to put my reactions on myself, my feelings, my anger, my hurt.

She looked hard at me, paused, and said quietly, "I'm truly sorry. I didn't realize I was coming across that way. I have so many patients at night. I'm under so much stress trying to do my job and care for all the patients." I told her I understood and I think she understood. When I left the hospital, we were good friends.

Working out a personality problem with a nurse can be difficult, but it's far less challenging than most of the situations I face each day. Hardest of all is communicating with a terminally ill patient. What can you say that's meaningful? What can you tell the family? How do you begin?

One thing I never do is walk into the room of such a patient and say brightly, "How well you look today." Such an approach after a patient has spent a night in pain, perhaps suffering physical and mental torture, can drive him crazy because he realizes that he cannot really communicate with you.

First I have to validate the patient's feelings, be there where he is. I can't express hope when the patient feels hopeless. I must put myself in his shoes. When I need to probe to find a way to encourage him to talk, I might open by saying, "You really look troubled today," and wait for his response before going further.

Of course you don't have to work in a hospital to face the problem of communicating with a patient. Imagine yourself visiting a friend who's had a heart attack. What do you say? Well, how about this: "God will help you. Keep that in mind and you'll have your health restored." No way. That's how many well-intentioned people might begin, but it's all wrong. It's not putting yourself in your friend's position. With that kind of opening, you might shut off communication entirely.

Let's try again. How would you feel if you were recovering from a heart attack? Probably you would have a lot of painful thoughts—the loss of health, the fear of dying, the possibility of facing a circumscribed life. Well, that's likely to be the way your friend feels. So, how's this for an opener? "What an adjustment you have to make! I don't envy you." Or, "I hear you saying, 'Who wants to live this way?'" Or, "I really understand how upset you must feel."

That's being there with the patient or with your friend. Remember, when you try to "make nice," you're not on his wave length and you can lose him. What he really needs is to express how rotten he believes life is, how he fears death, how he is concerned about taking care of his family, and so on.

As a clergyman, I have special considerations visiting patients with severe losses. The patient may want to vent his emotions but be reluctant to speak impious thoughts. Unless you know his true reaction to what's troubling him, you can't

help him. I encourage patients to express real feelings and
thoughts even if they fly in the face of my theology.

Being human, I sometimes slip and say the wrong thing.
Here's an example. Responding to an emergency call on my
beeper, I rushed to the bedside of a seventy-year-old woman
who was moaning with pain. She greeted me eagerly,
"Rabbi, Rabbi, I'm so glad you're here. Please come sit next
to me, Rabbi. Hold my hand." So I felt needed. She wanted
me and perhaps I could help her.

It was soon obvious that she was an uncooperative
patient. The nurse told me that she wouldn't take her
medicine voluntarily. I was there once when the telephone
rang. The nurse answered and said, "It's your daughter."
The patient wouldn't speak to her. "I have nothing to say to
her," she shouted. "Hang up!" The nurse pleaded with her
to take the call but to no avail.

The patient turned to me. "Rabbi, I'm dying! Don't leave
me alone! I'm dying!" Well, I stayed with her for quite some
time but then had to leave. I told her that other patients were
awaiting my visits. "I know, I know, Rabbi," she said, "but
you've been so helpful to me. Please stay." However, I had to
go. And this is when I fell into the communication booby
trap.

"You know," I said, "I will be away for a while but God
will be with you." That's something I try never to say unless
it's appropriate for a particular patient, but somehow it came
out. She looked hard and long at me in silent and mounting
rage. Then she exploded: "*Bullshit!*" I felt bad and couldn't
get out of that room fast enough.

Later I had a better understanding of the woman's
bitterness. The nurse told me a truly tragic story about what
had happened the previous day. Members of the family had
visited her and, in her presence, argued about who would
get what jewelry. They were dividing the loot even before
she died. The woman kept pleading, "But I'm still alive!

What are you doing?" They had made her a nonperson. They had phased her out.

She desperately wanted someone to hold on to. That was why she clung to me and rejected her daughter. And here I went and blithely said, "God will help you."

Before you can communicate effectively, you must master the art of truly listening. Earlier I mentioned M. Scott Peck's seminal book, *The Road Less Traveled*, which I found very helpful. In it, he brilliantly and succinctly describes what listening entails:

"True listening, total concentration on the other, is always a manifestation of love. An essential part of true listening is the discipline of bracketing, the temporary giving up or setting aside of one's own prejudices, things of reference and desires so as to experience as far as possible the speaker's world from the inside, stepping inside his or her shoes."

True listening has its spiritual component as well. When you allow another person to express himself without threat, you give him dignity, a feeling of control, and a sense of freedom even if all external circumstances deny his freedom.

To my mind, just as the so-distant sun with its hidden physical energy streaming through the universe nourishes the flower that turns toward it and opens its petals, so the sunlight of God's hidden spiritual energy and presence, the stream of his loving-kindness, nourishes and strengthens one's soul, opening it up like a flower in all its beauty.

So that when you give that kind of dignity to the patient, to your friend, to your mate, and he or she listens to you in turn, both of you dip into that spiritual energy stream and nourish each other.

That's how I survive burnout in my hospital rounds. I grow as the patient opens himself up to me. And I haven't found any patient who doesn't have spiritual problems. No one wants to be a zero. Everyone deserves to count, to have zeroes with numbers in front. When a patient suffers terminal illness, he wants to feel like a person, have some sense of what is going on, and to set things in order.

One of my hardest tasks is to help a terminal patient face the prospect of death. Before I can do this, I have to be able to discuss the subject with him. Sometimes the patient is ready but members of his family are not.

This story was related to me by a rabbinical student whom I'm training to serve as a chaplain. One of his patients, a man from an Orthodox Jewish family, was dying. The patient's brother, learned in the Bible, would never allow anyone to discuss death in his brother's presence. He told my student, "You've got to encourage him. You've got to pray with him."

One day the student chaplain came into the room while the family was huddled around the patient. "Please come another time," they told him. The next day the family was there again. This time the patient whispered to his brother, "Have everyone leave. I want to speak to the rabbi." Reluctant to depart, his brother asked, "Do you want anything?" Mustering whatever strength he had, the dying man said, "Yes, I want *you* to leave."

Now the young chaplain was alone with the patient, who asked him, "What do you think will happen to me?" The student had learned the proper response and replied, "What do you think?" The patient, disappointed, said, "I don't know," and repeated, "What do you think will happen to me?"

Taking up his courage, the student said, "I think you're going to die." The patient smiled and asked the young rabbi to pray with him. Together they said a confessional prayer. You don't often hear of Judaism being a religion of confession, but we do have a confessional before death. It says, in effect: "God, please hear me, healer of all flesh. If, in your wisdom, it is decreed that I am to die, please forgive me all my sins. Take care of my family and loved ones." When the prayer was over, the patient grabbed the rabbi's hand and held it close. Finally, he said, "Thank you for helping me say good-bye."

Sometimes you have to communicate by being silent, by sharing pain, by listening, by empathizing. The heaviest heartache involves terminally ill children.

What do you tell parents whose children are hopelessly ill? There is no one answer—if there is any answer at all—to assuage the pain. Sometimes I feel so inadequate. But I'm there with the parent who lets me in. Some parents are so angry that they won't speak to me, especially if they see me as representing God when God means only injustice to them.

Frequently the only answer is to come into the room, stretch out my hands, and hold on and cry together with the parents. If I come in when the child is feeling better, perhaps in remission, I play with the child and rejoice with the parents as well. The worst agony is the terrible disappointment if the remission fades and the illness takes hold again. I try to be present at that time to give a measure of comfort.

Etched in my memory is a scene of Lucille, a three-year-old girl, hooked up, stuck with IVs, lying limp like a Raggedy Ann doll, and her mother in mask and gown and sterile gloves hovering lovingly and bravely over the child. I knew how the mother had been struggling because I'd been sweating it out with her and weeping with her.

"How's Lucille today?" I asked. "And how are you?" The mother answered, "I'm holding on. It's so hard." So what do I say now? How can I bring comfort or strength? Words cannot do this. As I was leaving the room feeling impotent rage and grief, the mother embraced and thanked me. How did I help? The answer is I was there caring and weeping, and sharing feelings; sometimes nothing else can be done. Just by being there I took the mother out of her isolation and held her hand.

Yes, there are times when words are completely inadequate. This was brought home to me again recently. As I was leaving the hospital one evening, I was stopped by the husband of a patient I had visited earlier. He was distraught. "My heart is broken," he told me. "The doctor just broke the news. My wife is terminal. There is nothing more they can do for her. What shall I do, Rabbi? My wife is dying. There is no hope."

I sat down with him in the hospital lobby and stayed with him for two hours as he poured out his grief, his anger, his guilt, and his tears. I held his hand and I wept with him. I was with him as he laid bare all his emotions and his anguish. "Thank you," he said. "You've brought me comfort." What did I do? Nothing, and yet everything. I was there and just listened.

From my personal experience, I know how helpful another caring human being can be. When my first wife became ill, the greatest comfort was brought to me by the president of our congregation. He came and was there with me, saying very little, and I felt I was not alone. It gave me strength and courage. You, too, can offer others this gift of comfort in times of grief.

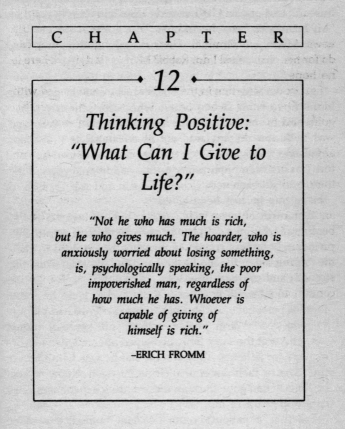

• 12 •

Thinking Positive: "What Can I Give to Life?"

*"Not he who has much is rich,
but he who gives much. The hoarder, who is
anxiously worried about losing something,
is, psychologically speaking, the poor
impoverished man, regardless of
how much he has. Whoever is
capable of giving of
himself is rich."*

–ERICH FROMM

If someone looks at life and says, "What can I get from life?" he's doomed to disappointment and frustration. There's no way he will ever be satisfied. But there is a different, far more rewarding perspective:

"I've been given so much. What can I give to life in return? How can I use my days and my years, my strengths and my abilities, to bring blessings to myself and to others as well?"

If you open your hands to give, you always receive a great

deal in return. Giving and taking, that's a lot of what life is all about. And nowhere is this more apparent than in my daily contacts with hospital patients.

The story of William, a very successful clothing manufacturer, is particularly memorable to me. William faced catastrophic illness, first in his family, then in himself. Recovering, he decided to retire from business and devote all his time to reaching out to others who were seriously sick.

William's son had contracted cancer twenty-five years ago, when cancer therapy was not as advanced as it is today. However, caring doctors in the hospital had helped him and he was given an opportunity to enjoy additional years of life. William had been very close to his son and was grateful for the respite he had been given.

A number of years later, William himself became ill with cancer, enduring a number of very debilitating treatments. Ultimately he was cured. At that time he resolved to show his appreciation for the healing and the life extensions that he and his son had received.

He volunteered as a hospital counselor. Here he found that his personality and his business experience had put him in good stead. Warm, affable, with a gentle sense of humor, yet serious at the same time, he helped open many windows of hope for patients. They sensed that he was with them in their fear or their anger or their depresssion. Knowing that he himself had gone through these searing experiences, they could open up to him.

Entering a patient's room, William immediately made contact by noticing the photographs on the dresser or the flowers in the room, or being aware of their absence. He would first relate to the patient from the point of view of his family and what it meant to him. Memories and little stories would follow. Before long, he became a friend.

The two strongest forces in his life, William once told me, were the love of his family and the love of his fellow man. He had learned to use his losses constructively. In touching others and bringing them nourishment, he received nourishment and growth in return. He allowed himself to be open, to give, and to take. And so doing he found his meaning through the kind of life he led.

His way of showing gratitude reminds me of the credo of Helen Keller, the American author and lecturer, who, despite being blind and deaf from age two, gained world fame for her aid to the handicapped. Helen Keller put it beautifully: "There is no lovelier way to thank God for your sight than by giving a helping hand to someone in the dark."

Although it may be more blessed to give than to receive, it is important to be able to take from others as well. Many people can't do this. One such person was Miriam, a member of my congregation, and a "giver" all her life. When she became ill, she was most distressed because she could no longer serve others.

"With all the treatments I'm getting," she once told me, "I don't have the energy to do everything, and it disturbs me." She was a meticulous housekeeper and prided herself on that, but now she didn't have the strength to maintain her high standards.

"Do what you can," I told her. "When you're tired, lie down and enjoy the rest. Think about how much your husband loves you, and about your love for him and your children. Just let your mind be at ease and relax."

She thought that was good advice but found it hard to follow. One day she got out of bed, staggered as she dressed, and with her remaining ebbing energy, went shopping. She stocked the refrigerator to save, as she put it, her "hard-working husband" from having to do it. When he came home and found her lying exhausted in bed, he was very angry with what she had done and berated her. Miriam told me how upset she was with him for reacting that way.

"Rabbi," she said tearfully. "He just doesn't understand that I *have* to give. I can't take from anyone. I've given all my life. Not to be able to give will kill me. I feel like a nothing, a nonperson."

I put my arm around her. "Miriam," I said, "by taking you are also giving. By letting go, you are giving your husband more responsibility for your well-being. You're saying to him, 'I'm happy to receive your love and that means everything in the world to me.'"

So far I've written about giving by adults. Yet probably one of the most moving and inspirational examples of giving in my personal experience came from a sixteen-year-old boy named Matthew Seegul. Matthew was seriously ill. His parents knew that he had only a slim chance to survive. Every time his cancer was contained by radiation or removed by surgery, it appeared again in another part of his body. Every effort led to a brick wall. Only a miracle could help— but no miracles were on the horizon. His parents grasped desperately at every straw. The staff searched valiantly for solutions.

Matthew himself turned out to be a miracle. Everyone on the floor—doctors, nurses, the hospital help and volunteers—were drawn to this valiant young man. Despite every debilitating treatment, he came back fighting with indomitable courage.

During the months of his remission, he returned to the hospital as a volunteer, visiting the children, bringing a smile to their faces, giving them and their families hope and courage.

News of Matthew's outstanding volunteer work even reached New York's City Hall. Mayor Edward Koch contacted Matthew's parents to arrange the presentation of a special medal to this praiseworthy young man. However, Matthew felt that he had done nothing special. His parents had to convince him to accept the award.

Since Matthew was now too weak to travel to City Hall, the mayor came to the hospital. Parents and staff stood there weeping unabashed in pride as the mayor, all smiles, presented the medal to Matthew. Matthew died soon afterward.

Matthew had been special, and his friends appreciated him. They knew he had been a hero. He had carried on bravely when he was so sick, editing the school newspaper, earning A's in his courses, and receiving science awards. And yet he was always just a regular fellow and a good friend who could joke around.

Although Matthew's chronological age was only sixteen, he was more mature in the depth of his wisdom and the strength of his character than many adults. Summarizing his outlook on life, he wrote the following essay which, I believe, could be read for profit by every teenager and every adult too. The wording is simple but the message is powerful:

What do dropout rates, drugs, teen suicide, and underachieving have in common? Give up? That is the point. They are all forms of giving up. The problem is that too many young people are giving up on their lives before they have lived them.

What seems to happen in these cases is that some goal seems so impossible to the individual that he or she just stops trying. What is forgotten is that the only sure way of losing at everything is giving up. A good example of what can happen—when people simply refuse to give up—is the Mets' battle against the Boston Red Sox in the 1986 World Series. After the second game, victory seemed ridiculous. But because they refused to give up, they were able to come back in the final two games and be victorious.

It is true that the life situations that cause teenagers to give up are complicated, but there are things we can do. We can change ourselves and our goals. We can get help. On these issues our situation is the same as the Mets. First, we must try so that we can stay in the game long enough for positive things to happen. Second, no one else will help us if we are not trying. Why should anyone else care about us if we do not care about ourselves?

Once we have straightened ourselves out about trying,

we have to do the same thing with others. First, who will support us in going after an attainable goal? Those people are the ones we want to know that we are trying. Forget about those people who either do not care or who are threatened by our achieving our goals.

The only cure for thinking of a glass as half empty is to learn to think of it as half full. The only cure for giving up is to hold on and always continue fighting. To borrow a line from Yogi Berra, "It's not over until it's over." So please, do not give up!

Matthew's parents established a special memorial fund for him and dedicated a room in the hospital in his memory. They mourn him and miss him. He was an only child. Though years will pass and "time is a great healer," he will always be remembered with a smile and a tear. The ache will remain but his presence will always be felt by everyone who came in contact with his splendid spirit.

His life was a gift. He made this world better for having passed through it.

I've heard people say they are tired of giving. "How long will I have to give?" they ask. The poet Edwin Markham answers that question magnificently:

> "Giving is living," the angel said.
> "And must I keep giving again and again?"
> My selfish and querulous answer ran.
> "Oh, no," said the angel, her eyes pierced me through—
> "Just give till the Lord stops giving to you."

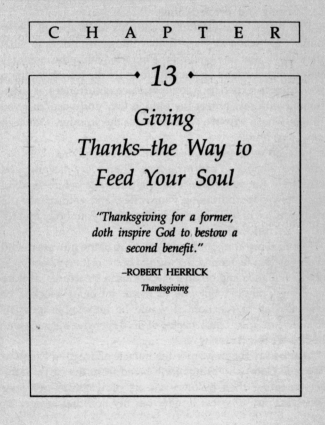

CHAPTER

• 13 •

Giving Thanks—the Way to Feed Your Soul

"Thanksgiving for a former, doth inspire God to bestow a second benefit."

–ROBERT HERRICK

Thanksgiving

The Jewish concept of sinning holds that one of the principal sins is not to be grateful for the blessings we have—when we have them.

This is just one aspect of sinning, but it is a very critical one, because it deals with how we look at life and how to make the most of moments that can never be repeated. And all these moments are steps to the sanctification of life, making it holy, if you will, making it fulfilling and complete. Or wasting our precious time.

Part of Jewish philosophy—and this holds true of Christianity and Islam as well—is that things are not only what they seem, that one can find the miracle within the everyday part of our lives and be thankful for it. In the Jewish tradition we strive to experience commonplace occurrences as spiritual adventures, to feel the hidden love and wisdom in all things. That's why we thank God for the wonders that each new day brings.

Judaism is, in part, a discipline of thanksgiving. Let's say you are religious in a formal sense. Then every morning you take time for meditation and thanksgiving before reading your newspaper, drinking your coffee, and getting into the daily routine of life. Grateful for the gift of your body and for all of its functions, you say:

"Praised are You, Lord our God, King of the universe, who with wisdom fashioned the human body, creating openings, arteries, glands and organs, marvelous in structure, intricate in design. Should but one of them, by being blocked or opened, fail to function, it would be impossible to exist. Praised are You, Lord, healer of all flesh who sustains our bodies in wondrous ways."

When I say the prayer for the miracle of bread—"Praise to Thee, O God, who brings forth bread from the earth"—the act of eating then becomes an act of worship, not only satisfying my physical hunger but my spiritual hunger as well.

I think for the moment of all that has gone into the miracle of this piece of bread. There was the earth, the hand that prepared the soil, the seed with its divine power of growth, and then there was the sun and the rain. The wheat was tended by man, cut down, ground, packaged, and transported to the baker who made this bread.

So when I say, "Thank you for the miracle of bread," it joins me with the cosmos. It bespeaks nature's miracle and

God's loving-kindness behind it, and for man who improved upon nature's product. That's what I mean by taking a commonplace act and becoming aware of the miracle that is there. And, from there, comes the sense of thanksgiving.

Now the sense of gratitude and being aware of the blessings is very different from having the blessings and not being aware of them. I like to illustrate this fact with the following parable:

A little girl is sleeping upstairs near an open window on a summer day. Suddenly a storm breaks. Thunder crashes and lightning flashes. Sheets of rain pelt through the open window. The mother, who is downstairs, realizes that her child is exposed. She runs upstairs as fast as her feet can carry her. Wind is blowing the curtains wildly. She runs over to the child, closes the window, pulls the cover over her shoulders, wipes her forehead—the child is still asleep—bends and kisses her.

Now let's take another instance. With the rumbling thunder and the shafts of lightning, the child awakens in terror and is screaming. The rain is coming through the open window. The mother runs up, closes the window, embraces the child, tucks her between the covers and kisses her. The child goes back to sleep.

The first child, who didn't awake, received a blessing but was completely unaware of it. Nothing changed in her life. The other child who was frightened received love and was awake to that love. The blessing that she received will always have an impact upon her.

The difference between being aware of our blessings or asleep to them makes all the difference in the world. Perhaps if we have the discipline of saying "Thank you," or reviewing in our minds before we go to sleep those things in our lives for which we should be grateful, it might affect the kind of lives that we lead.

If we are aware of our blessings, perhaps we would reach out to others who are deprived or need our love. Perhaps we've been too busy to extend ourselves, whether at home or in the workplace. It's important to remember that everybody is seeking the same kind of dignity and love that we're seeking.

Rabbi Joseph B. Soloveitchik, a great scholar and philosopher, cites another aspect of sinning—one that may surprise you. Pointing to the Jewish ritual ceremony after death of a loved one, he says it is an atonement ritual for the one who remains in life. The atonement, according to Rabbi Soloveitchik, is for the fact that we are creatures of hindsight and that is a sin for which we feel terribly guilty.

You may ask, "Why didn't I say I love you when the person was alive? Why didn't we go on a vacation? Why wasn't I there to meet her needs? Why did I say a word which hurt?" And then, when you look back, you may say, "Oh, this person was wonderful in so many ways and now I feel so alone. A part of me has been taken into the grave. Why, oh, why, wasn't I more appreciative when I had the time?"

Making the most of our time means that we appreciate our blessings while we have them. In appreciating them, we grow. Realizing that losses will occur, that this is part of life, we will be able to use these losses creatively. In the worst moments, when life overwhelms us with pain and sorrow and separation, we know and recall that there were good times, and have faith that they will return as we go through the darkness of the valley of the shadow.

And we don't have to look very far to count our blessings. This is borne out in Martin Buber's classic rendition of the Hasidic tale "Hidden Treasure." He relates the story of Eisak ben Reb Yekel, a very poor *melamed*, a Hebrew teacher, who lived in Cracow, Poland, long ago. With many mouths to feed in his family, with many bodies to clothe, he always struggled to make ends meet.

One night a strange dream was to change his life. He dreamed that in the distant city of Prague there was a great castle alongside a tall bridge. And under that bridge was a buried treasure! At first he paid no mind to the dream. But when it occurred the very next night, he began to take it seriously. Perhaps it was a signal from heaven that a far-off treasure did indeed await him.

The next morning he put a shovel over his shoulder, bid good-bye to his wife, and set out on foot for the long journey to Prague. After many weary hours he approached the outskirts of the city. And there, in front of his eyes, loomed the castle of his dreams and the bridge. Despite the fact that guards were patrolling the bridge, he took out his shovel and began to dig.

One of the guards left his post to inquire what this bedraggled man was doing. Innocent of guile, the *melamed* told him about his dream. The guard looked at him in amazement.

"This is very strange," the guard said. "Like you, I have had a dream every night that I can't explain. I dream that in Cracow there lives a Jewish teacher with the strange name of Eisak ben Reb Yekel. This teacher lives in a broken-down hovel where there is an old stove. Under that stove there is a buried treasure. But, of course, I don't believe in dreams."

When the guard finished talking, the *melamed* said that he had urgent business at home and took his leave. He went straight to his house, moved the stove, and began to dig. Lo and behold, there was the treasure and he became the richest Jew in Cracow. With part of his money he built a magnificent synagogue which fellow Jews always referred to as "Eisak ben Reb Yekel's shul."

Here is how Martin Buber explains the meaning of this parable in his *The Way of Man:*

> If we had power over the ends of the earth, it would not give us that fulfillment of existence which a quiet devoted relationship to nearby life can give us. If we knew the secrets of the upper worlds, they would not allow us so much actual participation in true existence as we can

achieve by performing, with holy intent, a task belonging to our daily duties. Our treasure is hidden beneath the hearth of our own home.

Yes, close to home are the treasures we possess if only we perceive them and are grateful for them. In this regard, I was fascinated to learn recently that a Japanese school of psychiatry stresses the role of gratitude in achieving good mental health. Under this therapy, called Naikan, a patient spends a week virtually alone in a room, speaking only to the therapist, who visits him several times a day. Each day the patient recalls, with gratitude, the kindnesses he received from his parents, his teachers, and others—and recalls, as well, his prior ingratitude in return.

Interviewed in *The New York Times*, David Reynolds, a psychotherapist who wrote *Naikan Psychotherapy*, the only book in English on this subject, said this method of treatment is "a way to honor the basic love and nurturance we've gotten from our parents, teachers, mentors—all the people who have helped us along the way. . . . It is a prod to purposeful action, self-sacrifice, and a gratitude that expresses itself in service."

Giving service is a touchstone of Jewish philosophy. In a sense, we have a covenant with God. He created us. It's the gift he gave us and we are supposed to give to life our fullest, which means doing our duty, doing it in a way that reaches into ourselves, and out to our fellow man, creating and shaping this world.

As the Bible states, "it's not good for man to stand alone." Man must reach out and, in reaching out, he takes responsibility for his life and he touches others. The good feelings that result are akin to feeding one's soul.

Judaism speaks of the mitzvah, which means both a good deed and a commandment. Regardless of how you feel, you are required to do the right thing. You don't feel like giving charity? Well, you *have* to. It is your duty and responsibility. Why? Because you are a guardian here for God and His wealth. You are required to share with others who are less fortunate.

G. K. Chesterton has said that the difference between the poet and the philosopher is that the philosopher tries to get the heavens into his head but that the poet tries to get his head into the heavens. For Abraham Joshua Heschel, the great Jewish philosopher, the whole routine of thanking God for His blessings is to awaken our feelings of poetry and to be led to God. The very fact that one can reason, says Heschel, regardless of where we think it leads us, should already awaken in us a wonder that leads to God. Heschel writes in *Man's Quest for God*:

> To pray is to take notice of the wonder, to regain the sense of the mystery that animates all beings.
>
> Prayer is our humble answer to the inconceivable surprise of living. It is all we can offer in return for the mystery by which we live. It is gratefulness which makes the soul great.
>
> As a tree torn from the soil, as a river separated from its source, the human soul wanes when detached from what is greater than itself.

By dipping into the stream of God's compassion in the universe, you make yourself open to it before crises arise. You also walk with the feeling of your own importance. In effect you are saying, "I am in the image of God. I'm the greatest, potentially. My life is a gift from God to me. So I've got to make the most of that gift and fashion it in the most beautiful way through my actions. To live up to my potential, it is my responsibility to bring God's design to its greatest fulfillment."

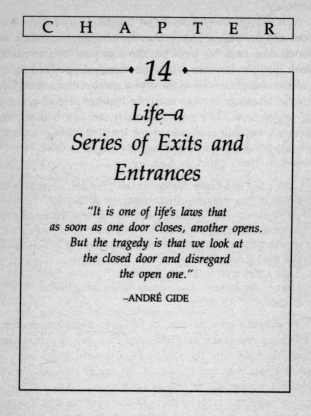

CHAPTER

• 14 •

Life–a Series of Exits and Entrances

"It is one of life's laws that as soon as one door closes, another opens. But the tragedy is that we look at the closed door and disregard the open one."

–ANDRÉ GIDE

As we travel along life's frequently rocky and rough terrain, proper perspective can bring stability and direction and help us avoid the inevitable pitfalls and potholes.

The enemies confronting us in loss and death are anger and despair. When a loved one dies, anger grows out of a sense that a terrible injustice has been done. I hear the cry so often: "Why do criminals, the riffraff, remain alive and healthy while my mate, who was so good, died? And how

he suffered. He didn't deserve it. Th
God."

When death occurs, we mourn the annihila
one. Our world lies in a shambles. Feeling forsa
lonely, it is easy to be frozen into a position of devasta
dark despair—a despair that disarms our defenses.

I know that feeling. From my wife's death I learned what
the pain of parting is, what loss means, what numbing
isolation is involved from community, from my fellow man. I
had to work out my own mourning. It took me a year to
overcome my grief, and I couldn't hurry it.

After the funeral and the burial, I had sat shiva (the seven
days of Jewish mourning), and friends and congregants
crowded my home. They had come to offer consolation and
then they departed, leaving my house quiet and empty. I
was painfully alone.

Good friends, sensing my loneliness, invited me to visit
them in Minnesota. I accepted the invitation, glad to get
away from the stifling emptiness permeating my home.
Their loving concern and presence, and the new environment, helped me bear the heavy burden of grief.

One evening they purchased tickets for a play, Tom
Stoppard's *Rosenkrantz and Guildenstern Are Dead*, and invited
me to come along. The play engaged my interest from the
very beginning. Halfway through the performance, the
Angel of Death appears and performs a duet dance with the
main character. I felt a powerful and strange hypnotic
feeling. It was like a magnet drawing me onto the stage and
into the dance with the Angel of Death. The rhythm, at first
slow and deliberate and then faster and faster, exploding
into wild, feverish, provocative movement, grabbed me.

Suddenly the dance stopped. The Angel of Death beck-
ons, fading slowly away. The stage is in complete darkness
except for the main character, who is now visible with the
powerful, bright spotlight illuminating only his face, for a

...t, and then suddenly, *pfft!*, the light flicked off,
...g a pitch-black void.

...e impact was overwhelming. One moment there, and
...e next gone. The effect upon me was shattering. I began to
...weep, my eyes flooding with tears. I couldn't control my
tears and I didn't want to. It hit me like a blow to the jaw. I
felt the emptiness, the loneliness, the nothingness, the
destruction, annihilation of life. I was swept up. I wept with
pity for all mankind and the tragic finitude of man.

The words of Ecclesiastes came to me: "Vanity of vanities,
all is vanity." And Job's anguished cry of resignation,
acceptance, came to my lips: "Naked I came forth from my
mother's womb and naked shall I return." It dawned upon
me later after reflection that my experience was like that of
Job, who challenged God's justice, and God appeared and
revealed to him the vast and incomprehensible mysteries of
creation and the universe.

I left that play with a disquieted feeling that I was on the
right path for resolving my grief but that I hadn't arrived yet,
that I had a way to go. It took me some time to sort out the
emotions and thoughts that were stirred by the play and
gain perspective. And then one day, as I was searching the
sources of rabbinic literature, I came upon it. There it was, as
plain as could be. Sometimes when you find an answer, you
say to yourself, "Aha! I've got it!" That "aha" feeling hit me.

I was reading a book by a contemporary scholar of Jewish
law and lore, Y. M. Tuckachinsky. It is called *Gesher Hachayim*
and is an important treatise on the laws of mourning. In this
seminal work, Tuckachinsky views life as a bridge between
the stages of birth and death, with an undisclosed destina-
tion beyond that bridge.

Tuckachinsky notes that the fetus exists, passive and
dependent, in the mother's womb, with no knowledge of the
fate before it, while the child that emerges is future-oriented,
possessing freedom of will to forge his life on the earth upon
which he has come.

The exit from the womb is called "birth" and the return to the mother earth is called "death." It is only life that is experienced in the present. So, says Tuckachinsky, this reality, this short stage of what we call "life," is our entire world, since we have no memory of the fetal past or knowledge of the long future that lies after life as we know it. He offers the following parable to illustrate his thesis:

Imagine twins gestating in the mother's womb, speculating and challenging each other with the question, "What will happen to us after we leave the womb?" Since their entire frame of reference is the interior of the womb, there is no way they could conceive through their sense of sight or hearing what their future holds in store for them.

Suppose that one of the twins is a "believer," supported by his traditions that there is a future life in the next world, while the other brother, a "rationalist," accepts only what his logical mind perceives in the here and now. They each take firm stands and debate their respective positions with passion.

Basing his argument on a religious tradition that he is heir to, the believer maintains that when they exit from the womb they will be reborn into a life that is not limiting, that they will eat through their mouths and not be fed through their navels, that they will see a great distance, that they will hear through the funny things on the sides of the head they call ears. Feet will be straightened and they will be walking erect great distances on this planet Earth, in which deep oceans and gentle streams flow, nourishing all living things. Above them will be the wide expanse of heaven containing a golden sun, a silvery moon, and twinkling stars.

The rational twin roars with laughter at his brother, the simpleton. "Incredulous! Are you for real? No one has ever come back from the other side to tell us. It's all a myth. All we know is what our senses perceive, the objective facts that can be tested. Aside from this womb and its limits, the rest is subjective and has no basis in reality. What do you think will happen when you die?" presses the skeptic.

"Clearly," his believing brother answers, "when we exit the space of this world, we will enter into another world."

"Fool!" snaps his brother. "You will fall into an abyss from which you will never return. You will be annihilated as if you'd never been."

Suddenly the water in the womb bursts. The rounded womb begins to shake and writhe. The believer makes a precipitous descent, is expelled, and gone from his brother's view.

The rationalist is shocked by his brother's fate and bemoans the tragedy that has befallen him. As he laments his brother's misfortune, he hears a piercing cry and loud shouts from the darkness into which his brother has disappeared. His fears of a terrible end are confirmed.

The skeptical brother is unaware that his supposed dead brother has entered into an exciting new world and that his own turn is near. The wail that he heard was a cry of a baby's health and the commotion was a chorus of congratulations from the doctors and nurses.

This parable opened for me a wide panorama with a distant horizon. It brought to mind the constant debates in our society between "believers" and "rationalists" on the question of life after death.

From the limited perspective of the fetus left temporarily behind in the womb, his brother had indeed died. He had been brutally torn from the familiar world that provided protection, warmth, and nurture and hurled into the black pit of oblivion and annihilation.

From a larger view, that same event is called "birth." It represents a transition from a smaller world to a larger world, from a world bounded by the womb, where all is passively received, to a wide, wide world where activity and free choice and responsibility open one to limitless possibilities.

The trauma of parting from the protected womb is necessary to enter the new and open world. In fact, that fetus could survive only by chancing the letting-go of one world to live and gain stature and dignity in the other. Now it became clear to me that this pattern of growing through the experience of exits and entrances does not just occur at the start of life. It is the pattern for all subsequent development.

Exits and entrances, before life as we know it and during life itself. Is it conceivable, I wondered, that what we call death is really a portal to another plane of existence? Here the Jewish tradition steps in. Rabbi Yaakov, an ancient Hebrew sage quoted in *The Ethics of the Fathers*, taught: "This world is a foyer which leads to the world-to-come. Prepare yourself in the foyer, that you may be worthy to enter the main hall. . . . One hour of bliss in the world-to-come is more exquisite than all of life in this world."

Thinking about life and death, I remembered reading that losses and sorrows are often the needles with which God sews our souls to eternal truths. I recalled the parable of the Dubno Maggid, a great itinerant preacher of the eighteenth century, who tells of a king who once owned the world's largest and most perfect diamond, of which he was justly proud. Whenever he felt depressed, the king would take out the diamond, look at it, and handle it. The diamond's brilliance, its pristine beauty, its purity thrilled him and elevated his spirits.

One day, as the king held the diamond, it slipped from his hand, struck the marble floor, and chipped. He was inconsolable. It was marred and he couldn't enjoy it as he had before. His advisors urged him to search out the most skilled diamond cutters from every corner of his realm to see if the gem could be restored.

Throughout the kingdom, the message was posted offering a great reward to the artisan who could make the diamond perfect again. But there was a catch. If the diamond cutter did not succeed, he would be punished with death.

The diamond cutters came and inspected the stone. But all agreed that it was impossible to restore it; the damage was permanent.

Sometime later, a craftsman from another land approached the king and asked for the assignment. "Not only can I correct the defect," the man said, "but I can improve on it." The king agreed to let him try but warned of the consequences should he fail.

When he finished the job, the worker brought the diamond to the king. The king's face lit up in a broad smile as he inspected it. "You have indeed improved on it," he said, "and the reward is yours." What was the craftsman's secret? Well, after cutting and polishing the diamond with rare skill, he made the scratch into a stem to which he linked a rose etched around the chip.

A deep truth spoke to me out of this parable. When someone or something bruises us, we can use the hurt to make our lives more radiant and more lovely. Despite its grim appearance, sorrow possesses vast potential power to deepen our understanding, sympathy, and courage, and to enlarge our visions.

In those heady days, another insight surfaced, rounding out my perspective. When my wife died, I felt that I had been robbed of a precious treasure. However, the prayer that I recited each day gradually began to change my bleak mood:

"God, you created the soul that you gave me, that you breathed into me. You return it to me each day after my night of sleep. Someday you will take it back from me. As long as I have breath, I shall thank and praise you."

And I dwelt on that as I stood swaying back and forth. My mind and heart were locked into that prayer. I meditated long and hard and recalled many memories, good and happy. The insight, simple but yet profound, came to me that life is indeed a gift to which I am not entitled and for which I should be profoundly grateful, and that I should respond by making every moment an opportunity for achievement, for paying back as a partner with God and creation.

This realization released me to divert all my pent-up energies, misdirected into depression and rage, into a channel of gratitude. I accepted a challenge to go on with and contribute in my life. A new sense of responsibility and empowerment surged through my being as I stood there.

My work in the hospital verifies this perception every day. Jack, a cancer patient who was dying and had come to terms with his death, once told me, "I have been occupied with what it is like to die and what will happen to me after death, and you know, Rabbi"—he smiled—"I am reconciled to death because I feel him as an old acquaintance."

"How so?" I asked, surprised by his reference to death in such personal terms.

"Well, Rabbi, you once asked, 'Jack, if you could reverse the reel of your life and play it over again, what would you change or do differently?' That started the wheels turning," he said. "I looked back over my life and came up with a surprising and comforting insight."

Jack then described the many good things he'd experienced and the hard knocks as well. Life is a mixed bag, but he had no regrets. He felt that he had lived a full life. Musing about the different stages of his life, he remarked that each move from a smaller world to a larger one had been scary, even when the occasion was a happy one.

He said it happened when he was taken to kindergarten and the teacher held his hand as he cried for his mother, who waved a tearful good-bye from the doorway. And when, at age thirteen, he stood with trembling knees on the platform of the synagogue at his bar mitzvah, chanting the Torah blessings and the words of the prophets in Hebrew. And again when he left for college, and years later when he stood under the canopy with his beautiful bride at his side. And when he reached mid-age and wondered, "Is that all there is to life?"

Most recently it happened when he received the bad news of his illness which turned his whole world topsy-turvy. "From all of this," he said, "I've learned something. Every exit is also an entrance. Every exit," he repeated, "is an entrance. When you walk out of something you do not walk into nothing unless that is what you choose. You walk into something else."

This patient's perception validated my own previous insight and helped me move out of my grief and despair and back into life again. Like Viktor Frankl, I recalled Nietzsche's words: "He who has a *why* to live for can take any *how*." That rang true. I was reminded of the sainted Hasidic Rabbi Levi Yitzhaq of Berditchev. Once he addressed God in prayer, "Mighty merciful Father, I endure so much pain and suffering. It is more than I can bear, and so does your persecuted people Israel. I don't question your righteous rule. I just want you to reveal to me why I suffer, that I can carry whatever burdens you place upon me and endure any test with which you confront me."

That image, that every exit is also an entrance, gave me a partial answer to the why. The concept of death as an experience of growth and transition and transformation rather than one of annihilation and destruction helped me to gain perspective. I felt as if I had awakened from a bad dream to a new day filled with promise and power and light.

I awoke the next day exhilarated, my blood tingling. As I stepped outdoors, bright sunlight greeted me in vivid contrast to the long darkness of grief. I shall never forget the moment. The sky was very blue, very clear, and very, very high. A faint breeze blew through the garden, cool and yet tinged with warmth. And everything—the skies above, the pavements, the buildings—was infused with the golden glow of sunlight.

As I savored that glorious moment, I was reminded of the prayer we recite for health, for healing of the soul and healing of the body. I felt that a heavy weight was removed from my shoulders. My soul had been released from bondage and from darkness to bask in the inner light of God's love. It was like a revelation.

I looked forward eagerly to the excitement of a new day. Previous sunny days were experienced as leaden, heavy, and bleak. This one brought me joy. I was filled with wonder and the excitement of new possibilities. The whole world was opening for me. I was in tears—and I was thrilled. My priorities took on a new order.

I had always wanted to paint, for example, so I began painting and attending a painting class. I also did some sculpting, another skill I had wanted to develop.

These were some of the things I did to make me feel fully alive again. And then I decided that it was time to reestablish a home and find another person to whom I could link myself in love. I had had a wonderful experience in a warm, close, home environment and I was eager to resume such a relationship.

I wouldn't go to singles' bars—that wasn't my style. So I contacted my rabbinical colleagues and told them I was ready. I also described some of the qualities I was seeking in a woman who would share my life.

The rabbis know the eligible women in their communities. One day a friend of a rabbi to whom I had confided invited me to a party where other single men and women were present. That's where I found Joan. It was almost love at first sight. Soon after, we were married and it's been a very stable, beautiful relationship.

My world had been closed off. Now new doors were opening and I went through them. Ever since our marriage, I have been, in a sense, on a high. By opening myself to this loving relationship, I dipped into God's mercy. My soul was fed, and that's a tremendous empowerment. I responded to life in all its fullness.

Truth to tell, I could not function now without burnout in the highly emotional, stressful environment of Memorial

Sloan-Kettering Hospital without Joan's support. We hear too much today about the breakup of the family. I want to sing the praises of a solidly based family, of the spiritual power generated by the family where there is harmony, respect, and the love of wife and husband for each other.

I sometimes tell the doctors I meet at Memorial that "I am part of your back-up team." Well, Joan is that back-up team for me. Alone, without her support, I do not think I could make it through.

The love with which she infuses our home, her sensitivity, intelligence and humor, remind me daily how fortunate I am, how the Almighty has blessed me. Out of gratitude alone, how can I not share that experience with others—of God's healing love which gives me courage, sustains and elevates me, and brings such joy and consolation into my life.

· 15 ·

Finishing Unfinished Agendas—the Path to Peace of Mind

"It is those who have not really lived—who have left issues unsettled, dreams unfilled, hopes shattered, and who have let the real things in life (loving and being loved by others, contributing in a positive way to other people's happiness and welfare, finding out what things are really you) pass them by—who are most reluctant to die. It is never too late to start living and growing."

—ELISABETH KÜBLER-ROSS, EDITOR
Death: The Final Stage of Growth

Generally it is considered a blessing if a person passes away quickly, without suffering, perhaps with a heart attack or an embolism. Yet sometimes I wonder—and this is hard to put into words—whether another kind of illness, where a person is warned and knows that his time is limited, is to be preferred, even with the attendant suffering, so he can complete his unfinished agendas.

Most of us go through our daily tasks leaving lots of loose ends to be tied up at a later date. That's when we have the luxury—or the illusion—of unlimited time on our hands. However, when catastrophic illness strikes, time takes on a new, diminished dimension. Completing our unfinished agendas becomes increasingly urgent. It is perhaps the only road to true peace of mind at this crucial time.

With critically ill patients, it is truly now or never. If they realize they have agendas to finish, relationships to resolve, rifts to heal, and summon up the stamina and the will to achieve these goals, they start living in greater depth. Life takes on meaning and the fear of death recedes.

Sometimes a patient's unfinished agenda is relatively simple, perhaps preparing a spouse for skills never before needed. I remember entering the room of Joseph, a forty-five-year-old man, asking, "How are you today?" He looked up at me and said, simply, "I'm terminal." I paused, collecting my thoughts. "What do the doctors say?" I asked, testing his sense of reality. He answered, "I've lived on borrowed time for two years. The doctors say nothing more can be done. I have a few weeks' time."

Letting that news sink in, listening, looking for an opening, I told him, "That's real hard, terrible news, but the doctors are not God, and many patients live beyond that time allotted to them." Then I asked him, "What are you doing with the time left that's so precious?"

"What keeps me going," he said, "is my concern for my wife. She doesn't know how to handle finances. I'm an accountant and I've always taken care of our funds and commitments. I'm doing my best to give my wife a crash course, to prepare her to lead her own life, to be in control, to provide for her security. And so I'm teaching her what has to be done, what accounts are here and there, and how the bills are to be paid."

Joseph spoke as a clear-thinking businessman, calm and unemotional. "I'm just doing my job," he said. "I'm a man who is very disciplined, very controlled, never shed tears. This is the way it is and I have to go on from there."

As he emphasized his responsibility to his family, I felt a tremendous admiration for him. And he saw that. I believe this helped give him an added sense of self-worth and dignity. "May I help you?" I asked. "May I say a prayer for you?" He said, "Yes, please."

I took his hands and held them. I recited a prayer and Psalm Twenty-three, "The Lord is my shepherd." A tear gathered in the corner of his eye and rolled down his cheek. The feeling was deep inside. Perhaps the recital of the prayer that released the tear also sent him the message that he was not alone, that he was connected with his people whom I represented, and with God as well.

When people hear they have a catastrophic illness, they react in different ways. Some immediately just shut themselves off from family and friends and life completely. They give up, and, before long, they die because, in a sense, they have willed it. But I'm speaking here of those who have courageously faced up to their situation and resolved to make the best possible use of their remaining time.

There was Harold, a successful entrepreneur who was a wonderful, kind human being. I had visited him several times before he told me he was terminal. After we talked for a while, he brought up a deep guilt he felt about a son whom he loved dearly but felt that he had wronged.

He had two sons who had grown up with quite different personalities and values. The older son was very bright but carefree. Something of a jock in college, he did a bit of carousing, and his grades were never up to par. Since graduating, he had held several jobs but never for very long. The younger son was highly motivated, very aggressive and assertive, and had shown a strong interest in the family business.

Harold owned a very profitable food manufacturing concern with many employees. He wanted to keep it a family business and brought in his younger son to work alongside him. The older son was excluded because the father believed he would ruin the business. Now he felt very guilty about that decision.

"I'd like to tell my son," he said, "that I love him, that I think he has a lot of ability but I didn't take him in because he lacked a certain discipline, and that it would be disastrous for him and the business if he failed."

"Why don't you tell him?" I asked. "Your son must think—" He interrupted me. "Yes, my son must think that I don't have faith in him, that I don't love him. Pesach, I have a terrible guilt." At this point I said, "Well, perhaps the time to tell him is now. If you do, drop the mask and be straightforward."

The next time I came into Harold's room his wife took me aside and told me that a wonderful reconciliation had taken place. The father had called the older son to the hospital. Recounting the conversation, she told me, "My husband said, 'I don't want to hide the fact that I'm dying. But I want to tell you, from the heart, how I feel about you. I love you. You know I've been upset about your college grades and your drinking. But I love you even when I criticize you. I haven't brought you into the business because I feel you're just not responsible enough. Maybe it's not right for you. Maybe you ought to be doing something else that really interests you.'"

The wife told me, "Our son looked at him, ran over to him, hugged him, and in tears said, 'Father, I understood that right along, even without your telling me. I always appreciated your letting me feel independent so that I could be myself and go my own way. Even though you didn't accept what I was doing, you accepted me. You did the right thing.'"

There were tears on all sides and much kissing. And there was a change that came over that man when I next visited him. He was at peace. He was no longer agitated.

Thinking about this man and other patients I have counseled always makes me wonder, why do we have to wait so long to finish our unfinished agendas? Why do we have to carry the heavy burdens of guilt, anger, and misunderstandings until the end of our days?

Families go through so much unnecessary aggravation, so much torment, so many failures of communication that tear them apart, so many unfinished agendas. It would be so different if we could accept the wisdom of Maimonides, the great rabbi, physician, and philosopher, who said we should look at each day as if it were our last. That way we would have to open up completely, drop all pretenses, and be right there with and for one another.

Sometimes it is hard to make contact with another human being. Esther, a woman with an unfinished agenda, refused to see me at first. When I visited her soon after she learned of her terminal illness, she told me politely but firmly, "Rabbi, I'm not religious, I've never attended services. Thank you, but I don't need your help."

However, her daughter, who was a schoolteacher, took me aside in the hospital corridor and urged, "Please, Rabbi, I have a feeling that you can be a comfort to my mother. Do try to reach her." Well, I tried harder and I succeeded. And I discovered that Esther was an amazing woman.

After several conversations in depth with Esther, I told her, "You know, you *are* religious in the sense that you have accepted the terrible illness and all the pain and terror that goes with it and are surmounting it. Not only that, but you are living vitally each day."

"What's the big deal?" she replied. "I've got so much to do. I'm concerned I'll never be able to finish it."

"You're a remarkable woman," I told her. "In a sense you're a mitzvah, a prayer in action. You inspire me and others."

"I don't know where I'm so great," she said. "My daughter also tells me how wonderful I am. Says she wishes she could have half my courage. Where's the courage? Things have to be done and I'm doing them. What choice do I have?"

"There is another alternative but, thank God, you haven't chosen it," I said. "You can pull the sheets over your head and give up. And there are patients who do that. They just die."

She just couldn't understand such a viewpoint. "How can someone surrender like that?" she said. "There's so much to do."

"You've found your meaning," I told her. "You are living life in greater depth than you ever did before."

"You know, you're right," she said. "I'm much more open to things, much more aware, much more sensitive, with so much more feeling."

Esther was completing her agenda and didn't want to leave her daughter with any part of it. I remember finding her hard at work at her sick bed with bills all over the table. "What's going on here?" I asked. She said, "Well, bills have to be paid and the bill collector won't be able to follow me." We both knew how short her time was and we both began to laugh. "Yep," she said with a twinkle in her eye.

There was never anything morbid about her manner. She never lost her zest for life and her compassion for others. Even when she hardly had strength to get around, she insisted on visiting patients. Many were the times I saw her holding a patient's hand and comforting him as he was wheeled down for treatment. The patients thought she was simply wonderful.

After she died, her daughter felt guilty that she didn't lessen her mother's pain by insisting that she be medicated heavily enough just to blank out. I reassured her. "Do you think your mother would have allowed you to take even a day of her life away from her, a life which was so precious to her? Do you think she would have given up even a moment of holding on to you, experiencing her love for you?"

She thought for a moment and nodded. "You're right," she said. "But losing her so soon after we really found each other is so unfair."

"Yes," I told her, "parting is painful. Unfair? Perhaps. But this I know—life is a gift, your mother was a gift to you. And this manner of parting slowly left her time to put her life into some form of relationship with God, with that stream of mercy and creation in the universe that's akin to love.

"She lived with an intensity that she never could have experienced without going through the valley of the shadow. It allowed her to drop all of her bitterness, to take life as a gift, the days as a gift, and your love as a special gift to her."

And I pointed out another gift. "When you were by her side when she died and you looked at her, was she at peace?" Wiping away a tear, she agreed. "Yes, she was at peace."

"You were there with her," I said, "and she will always be with you. And not only with you. Her life meant something special. It was a gift to the other patients. She showed her joy of living and her courage. I think that gave her a feeling of her own specialness, her own worthwhileness, which will persist in the memories of all who knew her."

Sometimes finishing an agenda means just continuing on the same path. I knew another woman patient who was actually the Mother Teresa type and even looked like her. Small, wizened, and dynamic, Sharon, a religious woman, was constantly involved in helping others. After she entered the hospital she received frequent calls from the outside social service agency with which she was affiliated. They constantly asked her advice—how can we meet the needs of this one who is suffering, or this one who is hungry, this one who is lonely? And she was always right there, even when her illness became difficult and painful.

We had many wonderful conversations. One day I said to her, "You're a religious woman. What do you think is going to happen to you when you die?"

Looking at me as though she felt this was a strange question from a rabbi, she said, "I'll go to the world to come."

"That's a place?" I asked.

"Of course," she replied. "That's where all the righteous people go and I hope I'll be righteous enough."

"What will you bring with you?" I asked.

Again she looked at me quizzically, surprised that a rabbi would question her thus. "Isn't it written in the works of our great sages that we will take along all our mitzvahs, all our good deeds?"

That's an example of completing an agenda. Despite her occasional great pain, her desire to assist in the healing of others, to be a partner with the Almighty, so to speak, helped her focus on the many tasks that still needed her. If, like Sharon, one has the faith and the point of view and perspective that this life will continue in some form in another world, it is, of course, a big plus in achieving peace of mind.

I remember two other patients that I met on the same day. One of them, a somewhat pompous man of about sixty, greeted me, "Oh, you're the rabbi." When I nodded, he continued. "Do you know this and this congregation and the rabbi there? Well, I'm very active in the synagogue. I'm president of the congregation and even helped build the building."

"That's very nice," I told him. "It must give you strength to face your loss of health and this life-threatening illness."

"Not at all," he said. "I no longer believe in God. I don't

understand why the decent people like myself who do all the good deeds get the shaft while the no-goods are out on the streets with drugs and mugging and murdering. No, with all the injustice around me, I can't believe in God."

I thought, "I guess some people consider him religious. They see him in the synagogue on Saturday as president of the congregation. But he has not internalized the teachings of Judaism. Or listened to the prayers that he himself recited." With no faith and no tasks to occupy him, he had very little support in his illness and was a bitter and angry man.

Another man that day said to me, "Rabbi, I'm an agnostic. I don't go to the synagogue. I don't know whether God exists. Maybe He does; sometimes it seems so. Please say a prayer for me because it makes me feel that there is someone up there who cares." This man, I felt, had more support in his struggle.

Thinking about the power of religion brings to mind a Hasidic rabbi patient who saw each day as a chance to set a new agenda. He took seriously his morning prayer that says, in effect, "You renew each day the works of creation and thus we have to be partners with God. He can't do it alone. We've got to improve His creation." Following the teachings of Judaism, the rabbi closed his good-deed agenda when night fell and opened it again the next morning.

During my time with this Hasidic rabbi I learned a great deal. Now, I'm a modern rabbi. No black coat or black hat. I come in a sport jacket when I visit patients. The rabbi knew I wasn't Orthodox. And yet, in my relating to him, he reached out to me.

When I entered his room, he would tell his fellow Hasidim, "Please stand, Rabbi Krauss is coming in." That gave me a sense of being in touch with my *neshama*, my soul. He gave me that feeling and it reinforced my knowledge that one human being can give that dignity to others.

He once said to me, "You know, we're all God's messengers. Even Adam, who rebelled against God and was driven from the Garden of Eden, was a messenger to have others channel into God."

"You are such a channel," he told me. "When you come in, I have a sense of shalom, peace, in wholeness, and you're there with me in my pain."

I think I shocked him once in a philosophical discussion when I asked, "What do you think of God for visiting all this misery on you?" He quickly answered, "God forbid that you should speak that way. I am being tested. And perhaps also being purified for some of the actions I have performed in this world."

Even though he was weak at the time, he never failed to participate at all religious functions. At one point his Hasidim received permission to use a hospital room to celebrate one of the happiest holidays in the whole Jewish calendar, the time of Rejoicing for the Torah.

It was a large room, and many, many Hasidim came. They sang and they drank and they ate and they danced. How they danced! There the rabbi was, enfeebled, but suddenly he gained the strength to carry a Torah. And the songs and the exaltation resounded up and down the hospital corridors. Everybody gathered around and rejoiced with the Hasidic rabbi.

Despite his illness, the rabbi was acutely alert and continuously active. When I asked the head nurse about his condition, she said, "I don't know how he survives. The doctors say he should have been long dead. According to the best medical knowledge, his survival is simply a miracle. Surely his faith sustains him."

CHAPTER

• 16 •

Coming to Terms with the Inevitable— Accepting, Coping, and Transcending

*"The hour of dying is only one
of our hours and not exceptional; our being
is continually undergoing and entering
upon changes that are perhaps of no
less intensity than the new, the
next, and next again, that
death brings with it."*

–RAINER MARIA RILKE
The New Book of Original Quotations

A comforting reality took shape within my mind and heart following the death of my beloved mother. I realized that I did not earn my way into this world into which I mysteriously came, nor could I say that I possess the people who have touched and influenced and transformed my life. It became clear that my mother had been a gift from the beginning. How fortunate that she came into my life, and that I came into hers. How undeserving I was of all the love with which she surrounded me and nurtured me, and how often I was oblivious to her blessed presence.

If we have the perspective that life is a treasure of time which gives us the opportunity to accomplish and to experience, then we can better accept, cope, and transcend when that gift is ultimately returned to the source of life. Then it is not seen as a defeat but as a summation, a conclusion.

In the words of Abraham Joshua Heschel, who had a strong influence on me, death is an "ingathering, the harvest of eternal moments achieved while we live." He continues: "We don't know how to die in grace because we do not know how to grow old gracefully. Growing old must be a process of cleansing the self, a way of getting ready for ultimate confrontation. If life is a pilgrimage, death is an arrival, a celebration. The last word should be neither craving nor bitterness, but peace and gratitude."

I can think of many patients who achieved that state of grace. One was Sylvia, a sixty-nine-year-old woman, a former schoolteacher, who was terminally ill. One day, when I walked into her room, she looked me straight in the eye and said calmly, "Rabbi, I'm dying."

Not sure of exactly how to respond, I waited for her next words.

"The doctors say they can do no more," she told me. "I'm ready. I have no regrets. I've raised a fine family, a daughter and two sons. They're grown now and well able to solve their own problems."

Here was a woman who faced reality serene and unafraid. To her, I would not try to extend false hope or speak in platitudes. "Were you open with your family?" I asked. "This is the time to drop all masks and say what has to be said."

"Oh, yes," she said. "I was open. I didn't lay a guilt trip on anyone. I was positive. I didn't want to be like my friend who died recently. Her husband lied to her and told her that she'd be coming home soon and she pretended to believe him. They lied to each other, trying to ease the situation, but that was wrong. She died unable to speak to her husband about what was in her heart. I know, because I was her closest friend. I don't want that. I want to speak to my husband and my children and say everything that has to be said."

Sylvia told me that her son, a physician, had come in from Oregon with his wife and their two children, had said their good-byes, and returned home. Her daughter, who had arrived from Israel, was staying with her father in Connecticut. They were coming to visit her every day.

"I feel bad about that," she said, "and I've requested that they move me to a hospital in Connecticut near my home to make it more convenient for them. That's the way to make it easier, not by cutting off communication. Rabbi, I've lived my life. I'm ready to die."

Deeply moved, I took her hand and asked if I could give her a blessing. She nodded. "May the Lord bless you and keep you," I said, and we recited Psalm Twenty-three together.

Saying a final good-bye to one's children is perhaps life's most terrible moment. That prospect loomed for another patient, Rebecca, a twenty-nine-year-old mother of two. She had lost her hair as a result of chemotherapy and looked wan and emaciated.

"I just can't bring my son and daughter to see me looking so bad," she told me tearfully. "They're only five and seven years old and wouldn't understand. I don't want them to remember me this way."

I felt that she was making a grievous mistake. "It's not enough to speak to them on the phone," I said. "Have them come to the hospital. Let them see you and hug you. Let them bring their toys and sit on your bed and play with you. They miss you so much. And since you feel your days are numbered—you hope that there will be many days but you're not sure—don't let this opportunity go by."

She thought for a moment, dabbed her eyes with a handkerchief, and agreed. "You're right, Rabbi," she said. "I'll dress up for them."

When I came to her room the next day, I almost did not recognize her. She was dressed in colorful pajamas and robe, wore makeup, and her head was covered with an attractive kerchief. As I spoke with her, the children were brought up. They ran to Mommy and kissed and hugged her and she hugged them tightly.

Rebecca died a few days later. But I knew how much it had meant to her to have been able to be with her children before the end.

Coping with the approaching death of a parent is another of life's most trying times. Sometimes the most difficult decisions have to be made. I remember Sophie, a middle-aged daughter, who never departed from the hospital bedside of her terminally ill mother. She was there day and night, tending to her mother's every need.

Then, as it happens all too frequently, the day came when the doctors said they could not do anything more for the mother and asked that her bed be vacated for another patient. Sophie was devastated. How could she send her mother to die in an institution? She remembered how her mother had cared for members of the family in times of dire illness. She had taken them into her home. "She was so wonderful," Sophie repeated over and over again. "How could I do this to my mother? I could never forgive myself."

The doctor and the social worker were of one mind: the patient had to be sent to a hospice. I spoke to the social worker and asked for her evaluation. Unsympathetic and impatient, she insisted that Sophie was on a "guilt trip." I suggested that perhaps Sophie be given some additional time without heavy pressure and I offered to work intensively with her. The social worker reluctantly agreed.

I visited Sophie every day and encouraged her to learn all the facts so that she could make up her own mind and come to a decision. The question was whether she would be able to take care of her mother and all her specialized needs. It had to do with medication and special tending and whether it could be done at home.

Given the time and space, the solution finally presented itself. The mother improved somewhat. The hospital held her for a longer period. In the meantime, Sophie learned to take care of the dressings and medication. She arranged for practical nursing help and for a doctor on call for emergencies. And she brought her mother home.

The day she left the hospital, Sophie greeted me with a smile and a hug. Later she sent me a warm note expressing her gratitude for my help in strengthening her resolve to let her mother spend her last days in her own familiar loving setting.

Following the loss of a loved one, new bonds must be forged to face life under the changed circumstances. This was the case with Mildred, whose husband died after a long and harrowing illness. I had visited them often during his hospital stay and I was struck by their very close, loving, and supportive relationship.

A month after her husband's death, Mildred called me. The passage of time had not brought comfort. On the contrary, she did not know how to relieve her anguish and pick up the broken pieces of her life. She wanted to know if she could speak with me.

When we met, Mildred expressed her bewilderment and her suffering. I empathized with her. I assured her that the working out of the grief was normal but painful. She had been so close to her husband that it would surely take time to heal the breach. I suggested that she begin forging another linkage and asked whether she was ready to make the attempt. She said she did not know where to begin.

We explored her interests and I suggested she might

consider visiting the hospital as a volunteer or joining
Hadassah or a local synagogue. She agreed to give it a try.
Since she lived in my area, I contacted the leadership and
some members of the various organizations and urged them
to reach out to her and make her feel welcome.

They telephoned her and invited her to meetings. Some
came to her home to accompany her to make it easier for her
to enter into an unfamiliar environment. In each case the
membership received her, welcomed her, and followed
through in supportive friendship. Mildred responded to
these overtures and exposures and was on her way.

Whenever there is the loss of a dear one, you may go one
way intellectually but emotionally you have been wounded
and the wound has to heal. There are no shortcuts. Everyone
has to work out the mourning process with its accompanying psychological undercurrents.

When the bad news is received, the survivor is frequently
numbed into a sense of shock and disbelief. Almost univer-
sally, a person will voice a variation of, "It's like it's not real. I
expect him to walk through the door. I pick up the phone to
speak to him. I go to the stove to prepare his dinner."

After the death of a loved one, we have to free ourselves
from the darkness of hobbling memories of a past that
cannot be relived and emerge into the warm sunlight of the
present. With acceptance comes healing and opening up to a
new way of life.

This is illustrated in the book of II Samuel (12:15–23),
which tells of the time when King David's infant son was
deathly ill. For seven days David concentrated on praying to
God for his son's recovery, refusing to eat or perform any of
his regular duties. When his child died, his servants wondered how to break the news, fearing his reaction. However,
when David saw them whispering to each other, he realized
what had happened. To his servants' great surprise, he
immediately resumed his normal life. David explained that
he had done everything he could to forestall the dreaded

outcome but, once it had occurred, his perspective changed. Now his responsibility was to find ways to follow the trauma of loss with a meaningful form of existence.

King David's example can be a beacon for all of us. Life is a series of losses and we have to use these losses constructively, not only to cope but to transcend and, beyond that, to grow in understanding and in depth.

• 17 •

Grief–Healing
the Most Painful
Hurt

*"All of mankind is of one Author,
and is one volume. When one man dies, one chapter
is not torn out of the book, but translated into
a better language; and every chapter must be
so translated. God employs many translators;
some pieces are translated by age, some by
sickness, some by war, some of justice;
but God's hand is in every translation,
and His hand shall bind up all our scattered
leaves again for that Library where
every book shall lie open
to one another."*

–JOHN DONNE

Saying the last good-byes and parting from a loved one is always heartrending. There is no easy way to let go. These terrible moments can shake the very foundations of our theology and wreak havoc on our spiritual and emotional lives. However, the pain can be lessened if the patient and those close to him prepare themselves for the inevitable.

There is a profound distinction between a "good" and a "bad" death. In good deaths there is complete and open communication from the very beginning. And there is closure, with love expressed and experienced and forgiveness sought and given. This can make a great difference between "good" mourning and "bad" mourning.

Healthy anticipatory grieving begins to work its healing power when the family is truthful, open to the patient and to one another, and does not fall prey to what has so aptly been termed "the compassionate lie." Families may demand silence, conspiracy, and deception: "Doctor, don't tell him. He'll fall apart. He won't be able to take it. He'll just give up. He'll commit suicide." Such feelings are understandable but misguided.

In his highly regarded book *Coping With Cancer*, Avery Weisman reports that ninety percent of newly diagnosed patients want to know the truth. "Good coping," he writes, "requires that a patient have sufficient information to participate in decisions. Secrecy does no one any service. It bars effective communication and stalls coping. Moreover, an adult may feel abandoned, alone, baffled, apprehensive, as well as justifiably insulted at being left out. Desertion at moments of truth creates a distance that may be more devastating than the diagnosis. Distress is largely determined by *how* a patient is told about cancer, not what he is told."

Shielding the patient through the mistaken notion that he can't take it achieves an effect opposite to that intended. The patient and family are left dangling with unfinished agendas. Anticipatory grieving, vital to begin the healing process, is stunted. Unresolved emotional loose ends remain and guilt feelings extend even beyond death.

Even if there has been a lifetime of shielding one another from trouble and loss, the family must learn to operate on another level—dropping the masks and opening up channels of communication and love. They must resolve outstanding issues and provide the opportunity to say forgive me, I'm sorry, thank you, I love you, I believe in you and in your specialness and preciousness.

This gives the patient the chance to validate his life and to reinforce his sense of dignity and meaning. He can replay his memories as the family shares in them through laughter and tears of discovery and expressions of love and caring. If that process is cut off, the family is left without a chance to say good-bye. Should this occur, unspoken and unforgiven guilts may linger for years in recurrent cycles of unresolved grieving.

If you have the opportunity for anticipatory grieving and you are open to the patient, you grow and he grows and his last days can provide a quality existence. Then you can gradually let go even as you are holding tight. As you let go with open hands, so to speak, you embrace the dying person and bring the family together. This is especially true if you can be present at the last moment, when your loved one leaves the world. Such sharing in an experience that is part of the totality of living leads to a better bereavement.

Regardless of how well prepared a person is for bereavement, the work of mourning is a vital process which must be experienced to heal the wound. From my experience as a rabbi, a chaplain, and a man who has suffered personal loss, I have learned there is a way to provide strong support to a person who is in mourning. It's exemplified in the following poem—"Grief" by John Robert Quinn—that I read from time to time at funeral services:

> *Grief, being private, must*
> *be borne alone,*
> *And though I cannot share*
> *your sorrow, still*
> *Your anguished tears are*
> *mingled with my own;*
> *I walk unseen beside you—*
> *up the hill.*

> I can but hope that the pain
>   within your breast
> Will lose its sting, your
>   loneliness will melt
> When spring returns to meet
>   the yearly test,
> When on the pear the first
>   white blow is dealt.
> I shall not surfeit you
>   with vapid words,
> Claiming to know the
>   answers to it all;
> I only ask, so long as
>   darkness girds
> Your world, to let these
>   shoulders ease the fall.

"Grief" alludes to a special kind of relationship in which a true friend reaches out to a grieving companion. He offers to be alongside him in all his pain and misery. There is really little more that one can give to a bereaved friend. But it is a great deal. Not allowing a person who has experienced a great loss to walk alone is the greatest act of love that heals.

When a deep wound has been inflicted, a vital link broken, a dread loneliness settles like a dark pall, filling the mourner's whole being with a sense of hopelessness. That's when a true and wise friend is especially needed. If he can mingle his mourning friend's "anguished tears" with his own, if he can walk beside him "up the hill" in his lonely trek through the valley of death, if he can let his "shoulders ease the fall," he can provide a presence that can help heal the most painful hurt.

A mourner feels his greatest despair after sympathetic visitors disperse. His house is empty and his evenings frequently dreary and unbearable. That's when the steadfast friend who is there for the long haul fulfills the greatest need. His contribution goes far beyond his presence, important as it is. By being there, he encourages his friend to express his anger, guilt, and depression, and to openly shed his tears.

I know this well from my hospital experience. In my rounds I frequently help patients to cry. I tell them that greater strength is shown by weeping than by desperately holding back the tears. If emotions are repressed and bottled up, they can wreak havoc with a person's health.

Sometimes a child mistakenly interprets his parent's weeping as a sign of weakness. That was the case with my son, Jeremy, who was sixteen when his mother died. His love for her was overpowering and during her critical illness he guarded her bedside fiercely.

Jeremy was deeply wounded but did not outwardly mourn when his mother was laid to rest in the earth. Instead, he wrapped himself in an emotional cloak that cut off expression of feelings. I wept when I broke the news to him and couldn't stop weeping. It was the first time he had seen me cry. Jeremy saw my sobbing as unmanly, lost respect for me, and felt he could no longer count on me for support.

The strain of parting was just too agonizing for him. The stream of love that he had experienced was abruptly cut off. It was only when he was married and reconnected with that powerful flow that he was able to write to me about his new awareness about how my life touched his and how it touches others.

"I understand now that it was not weakness when you wept," Jeremy wrote. "I appreciate the fact now that you have a great deal of strength, that every time a door closed in your life, you opened other doors. Thinking about how you have transcended your difficulties helps me handle the crises in my own life."

A relationship that is accepting and allows for openness encourages a grieving person to pick up his broken chain and to forge new links with the living. Fortunate indeed is the mourner blessed with tried-and-tested nonjudgmental relatives and friends who stay on "so long as darkness girds" their world.

There are good and bad ways to deal with the trauma of severe loss. What never helps is the attempt to offer a rational explanation for the death of a loved one. This inevitably places an additional burden on a suffering family. Such tragic events are circumstances to live through with initial confusion and pain—and then to open into newfound courage and renewed hope.

The Book of Job illustrates this point. When Job suffers the loss of his seven children and his entire wealth within a short time, the shock triggers a breakdown in his health. When his friends come to comfort him, they hardly recognize him. He is a devastated man.

Putting on sackcloth and ashes, his friends sit with him, grieving in silence. For seven days they stay at his side and mourn with him. And Job is comforted.

Then Job cries out in pain. "Why did God inflict this on me? I have been a righteous man. Why this suffering?" The friends break their silence and begin to answer Job. They defend God, justifying the misfortunes visited upon Job. Deflecting Job from working out his grief which could lead to a new perspective and hope, they cause him to become fixated upon his rage and his despair. "Who did this to me and why?" becomes the focus of Job's lament. Instead, he should be asking, "What can I do now that this has happened to me?"

Job challenges God to appear before him so that he might present his case. When God makes his presence known, He rejects Job's "comforters." But He does not answer or explain by intellectual arguments. Instead, God reviews the vast mysteries of creation in the universe. Job is overwhelmed and responds, "I am speechless. What can I answer? I put my hand to my mouth. I've said too much already. I will speak no more."

Awe-stricken in the face of overwhelming dread and

beauty, Job says, "I will be quiet now, comforted that I am but thus." The mind and experience of man is too limited to grasp the mystery of life and death and creation. Man just cannot fit God's workings into his narrow perceptions.

In this regard, Maimonides once compared man's comprehension to that of a certain fish in the sea. This fish saw many fish disappear and never return. It was intrigued by the problem and determined to discover what happened to them. When the tide came in, the fish made a mighty leap and landed on the beach. It lay there flopping around and gasping for breath. The water receded and the fish died.

There's an important lesson in that little story. Maimonides is telling us that the fish can perceive things only through the limits of its sight and its natural medium, that of water. Once out of its environment, it perished. It could never know the world of the earth's atmosphere and thus is incapable of comprehending the total view, the entire panorama of life and death.

Job was diverted from his natural environment of faith by his friends. The explanations they provided would never have touched or helped heal his pain, his loss, and his bereavement. The core of his greatest challenge was to accept the inevitable, to gather his energy, and to continue living in his world without the presence of his lost loved ones.

Everyone who has gone through the ordeal of a loss knows how hard that is to do. But realistically, we have no alternative. It all goes back to the perspective that a loved one is a gift and we must be grateful that we had that gift as long as we did. That's a message I often bring to parents when I officiate at a funeral of a young child. I tell them the story from the Talmud of Rabbi Meir, a great pharisaic teacher, and his wife, Beruryah, a very brilliant woman. They were the parents of twins, dearly beloved children.

One day after Rabbi Meir went to the synagogue to pray on the Sabbath, something happened—we don't know precisely what—and his two children died in their crib. Beruryah placed both of them on a bed and covered them with a sheet.

At the conclusion of the Sabbath service, Rabbi Meir returned home. "Where are the children?" he asked. Attempting to ease his pain, Beruryah put him off.

"My husband, I have a question to ask you," she said, "about something I find very distressing."

"Yes," said Rabbi Meir, sensing her seriousness.

"A neighbor came a number of years ago and brought me a necklace with precious stones. 'Please keep this for me,' she pleaded. 'I am going on a long and dangerous journey. I place it in your keeping until I return. Will you hold it for me?'

"I agreed. I have come to love the necklace. It brings me great pleasure and has added beauty to my life. Now the owner has come back and wants to claim it from me. I cannot part with it. What shall I do?"

"The answer is clear," responded Rabbi Meir with some impatience. "It must be obvious that the one to whom it belongs should receive it in return."

Beruryah came close to her husband with tears in her eyes. "Meir, if you hadn't been so firm in your reply, I could not have returned that precious necklace."

She reached out, tenderly took hold of his hand, and led him to the room, opened the door, approached the bed, and removed the sheets covering the two children. Beruryah embraced her stunned husband. They stood there and wept, Rabbi Meir kept crying, "My sons, my sons."

Beruryah turned to Rabbi Meir. "Didn't you admonish me for growing so attached to the precious necklace and refusing to return it to its rightful owner?" The answer sunk in.

Rabbi Meir lowered his head in grief and cried out, "The Lord has given and the Lord has taken away," the words of Job. "Praised be the name of the Lord."

They embraced, stood there before their children, weeping their hearts out. And in their great grief they were reconciled to the tragedy that had befallen them.

As we go through life, losses are inevitable. Death, divorce, other separations may occur. And there is always the possibility of loss of health, loss of a job, and other losses, great and small. To transcend these losses and achieve a meaningful existence, hope, courage, and a proper perspective and outlook on life are all-important.

Something else is required—a leap of faith. To rebound from the pain and separation, we need the faith that life's blessings of the past—of which we are most profoundly aware when there are losses—will be renewed and experienced in even greater depth.

When we go through the painful and fearsome Valley of the Shadow of Death and loss, what we get back is a deepened and enlarged capacity for life, for flexibility, for gratitude, for sensitivity, and for trust. I have seen this happen to so many people in the hospital, and in my congregation and in my own life. But it is not automatic. Some people, as I have said, become bitter, others better.

Loss can embitter a person forever. I see people daily, among them some Holocaust survivors, who, experiencing pain and loss, say, "Never again. The agony is too great. I will not allow myself to open up again to others, to make connections and form new relationships which will expose my own vulnerability again to pain when love occurs and I'm rent asunder." They then close themselves off from everyone, from life, and shrivel up and die.

But I have also seen courage and growth stimulated by loss. Every day I see patients who straighten out priorities, who tell me how grief and loss have deepened and widened their ability to participate in life as they had indeed never experienced it before in the good days when they had health but weren't aware of its blessing. They have become more grateful for all these gifts of life, companionship, and love;

this world, with its music, art, and beauty, and everything it has to offer. These gifts are there and open to them now in greater intensity. They have become more sensitive to life's mystery and more trusting in their adventure with God or with life.

I speak of God in a specific sense. For those patients who identify the experience of exits and entrances, life is a gift from the divine. And for those patients who do not speak of or identify with the name God, who may even reject that name and existence but whose gut feelings are that they have found a new and profound meaning in their lives, there is a renewed sense of self-worth and dignity.

Any attempt to deal with tragedy by explaining it—as did Job's friends—is futile and counterproductive. Human relationships and faith—not unknowable answers—are crucial in working through a necessary period of mourning.

It is a mystery of God—or call it nature if you choose—that faith is the underlying principle of life. If we have faith and see loss as a prime and purifying thrust to growth, we will enhance our spiritual strength. We can then enjoy life in all its grandeur and fullness.

CHAPTER

• 18 •

Lighting "the Fire in My Bones"

*"Each of us possesses a Holy Spark,
but not everyone exhibits it to the best advantage.
It is like the diamond which cannot cast
its luster if buried in the earth. But
when disclosed in its appropriate
setting there is light, as from
a diamond, in
each of us."*

—RABBI ISRAEL OF RIZIN

The foundation for my faith was laid, in large measure, by a learned and caring rabbi who introduced me to the wonders of the Shabbat, the Jewish Sabbath.

The Shabbat is to feel a foretaste of the world to come. It is a day when we cease all striving in a material sense and all competition. Money is not handled. Contemplation rather than commercialization rules supreme. All the ends of life for which we work all week long—love, family, rejoicing, study, meditation, prayer, companionship—are beautifully tied together on that day.

Upon that Shabbat foundation, an extraordinary teacher helped build a religious structure for me that has grown taller and deeper over the years. It was that master who ignited the long-burning "fire in my bones." He also made me heir to a Hasidic tradition of "soul music", the *niggun*, that rises from the depths of my being to comfort me during times of trouble, and elevate me during times of joy.

As a youngster I had no idea of the spiritual direction I would take. Far more absorbed in sports than in religion, I had dropped out of religious school following my bar mitzvah. Three years later, when I was caught up in the exciting and heady experience as captain of my high school gymnastics team, my Hebrew school teacher sought me out and pleaded with me to return and continue my Torah studies. Politely and firmly, I declined. I had no time now and no desire. He departed disappointed. That meeting stuck with me, tucked into the back of my mind.

I graduated from high school still glorying in my athletic prowess. Despite the many changes in my life since then, I treasure to this day the senior class yearbook with the picture captioned, "Captain Krauss doing his stint on the high bar."

My life and focus changed irrevocably around this time when we moved from the neighborhood and I left my old friends who were obsessed with every form of sports. In my new surroundings I came into contact with a different group—vital young people whose dominant interests were Judaism and Zionism. They opened up a new world for me of which my parents were only faintly aware.

It was as if I had been dislodged from a secure but narrow space and propelled into a wide open, fascinating world. I guess I was ready for it because I gobbled it up. Like most teenagers, my physical and mental horizons were growing.

It was a time of idealism and dreaming of doing great things, of building a better new world.

This was also a time to experiment, to reach out for independence and break parental bonds and forge new ones for myself. That's when susceptible teenagers sometimes follow their peers into the dangerous world of drugs and sexual promiscuity, violence or even suicide. Fortunately, although I rebelled, I clung to certain of my parents' values. Not religious or well educated, they were honorable and hardworking people. I appreciated that and loved them.

I discovered that I hungered for spiritual sustenance and that my appetite was virtually insatiable. I fell in love with Hebrew, the holy language of the Bible, of my people, my God. My teacher's visit came to mind. No wonder he had pleaded with me. I remember him telling me, "Come back, Pesach. Study Hebrew. It is the key to the treasure house of your people's spirit." My whole being yearned for that treasure.

Returning to religious school, I began at the bottom. I threw myself into learning Hebrew with the same abandon I had shown in perfecting gymnastics techniques. After several years I reached the most advanced class. By then I was speaking Hebrew and studying biblical and rabbinical texts.

Together with a few of my class friends, I spent a summer studying the prophet Jeremiah. We studied on our own and enjoyed many exciting hours arguing the ethical and religious implications of this most personal and passionate prophet.

I remember feeling that Jeremiah's cry to God spoke to me personally: "Your words are like a fire within my heart shut up within my bones. O Lord, I weary myself to hold them in for I hear whispering against me of terror on every side" (Jeremiah 20:9, 10).

Jeremiah pleaded with his people to return to God and to a righteous path and in His name threatened destruction if his message were not heeded. And when his prophecy was fulfilled, the prophet who had been ignored and persecuted walked brokenhearted in chains with the remnants of his people on the way to Babylonian exile. "O," he wails, "would that my head were water and my eyes a fountain of tears that I might weep day and night for the slain of my people" (Jeremiah 20:16, 17). And there he begins to comfort them, to help heal their broken spirits, and to encourage them to carry on.

That summer I was there with the prophet and my people. It all came together when the Young Judea group of young Zionists came to me and asked me to lead a club of twelve-year-olds. They urged me to take an active part in the movement to rebuild the ancient holy land which God promised to Abraham and his children.

I remembered Jeremiah and I felt that "fire in my bones." To this ideal I could devote my life. I accepted the offer and became the leader of these kids. The first thing I did was to learn the "Hatikva," the national anthem of the Jewish people, so that I could sing along with the children who already knew it. I can't recall what kind of a leader I was, but I know that I was imbued with a flame of love for my people and Hebrew. Linking myself to my people's destiny and their dreams, I was ready to grow in leaps and bounds.

Another important linkage occurred around that time. Four of my friends—Bertha, Herb, Mimi, and Morty—were children of Rabbi Louis Feinberg of the local synagogue. One day they invited me to their home for the Shabbat. I had never experienced a Shabbat at home and looked forward eagerly to the occasion. I was not disappointed.

Sabbath eve finally arrived and I entered the rabbi's home and was greeted so warmly that I immediately felt at home. And then an evening began which changed my life.

I see it now in my mind's eye. There was the table set in the dining room with the white tablecloth, the finest dishes, the best silverware, the fixture lamps overhead, and the sweet, delicious fragrance of the Shabbat food filling the air.

We gathered around. Mrs. Feinberg and the girls lit the Sabbath candles, covering their eyes in meditation and then crying out, "Shabbat shalom," a peaceful Sabbath, and embracing each of us with a kiss. The evening began with a kiddush, the prayer over the wine, and proceeded with interesting, lively conversation, much laughter. Then came the singing of the Sabbath *zmirot*, traditional songs, and the singing of the grace after the meal.

By the end of the meal I was in tears. The esthetics, the beauty, the warmth, and the joy and love that permeated the atmosphere were overwhelming. God's presence was there. I felt a little like Cinderella, who was transformed into a princess by the fairy godmother and then went to the ball in the palace.

It became clear to me that Judaism is to be lived every moment of the day, every day—not just a theory or theology. My faith as a Jew was now to be grounded in a way of life, based on the mitzvah, the righteous act, connected with my God and with my people.

I went about actualizing that. I learned to chant the kiddush prayer over the wine and to sing the grace after meals. Fortunately the Feinbergs invited me often to their Sabbath meals. They saw how eager and hungry I was, not only for the food, which was delicious, not only for the young ladies, who were very attractive, but mostly for the spirit into which I was plugged and electrified and which elevated me.

In my spare time, I rehearsed the *zmirot* songs, the words and the music. They became part of me. I sing them each week at my Shabbat table and have passed them on to my children.

Rabbi Feinberg was a gentle, scholarly, caring person who left an indelible imprint on me. He went out of his way to feed intellectually a spiritually starving youngster. The model for my rabbinate in later years, he helped me take a giant step forward in discovering my meaning in life.

During this period, an extraordinary teacher deepened my feeling for and knowledge of Judaism. His name was Abraham Joshua Heschel. He was to become perhaps the leading Jewish philosopher of our day who influenced not only Judaism but Christianity as well. Professor of Jewish mysticism at the Jewish Theological Seminary, and a leader in the civil rights movement, he had marched hand-in-hand with the Reverend Martin Luther King in Selma, Alabama.

Dr. Heschel, who received his doctorate in Berlin, didn't know at that time that he was destined for greatness and neither did we teenagers who met with him to study holy texts on the Shabbat day as the sun was setting.

He had been a young scholar then who had replaced Martin Buber, one of the great philosophers of the twentieth century, as the director of the prestigious Lehrhaus College of Jewish Studies in Berlin. Dr. Heschel was one of the Jewish scholars saved from the Holocaust by the Hebrew Union College.

Dr. Heschel traced his lineage back generations to the holiest level of Hasidic rabbis and leaders. He carried within him its stories and *niggunim* (songs without words) created by these rabbis and holy texts.

A master of Western philosophy as well as biblical, rabbinic, and Hasidic tradition, Dr. Heschel was a unique phenomenon. His manner and the loving care with which he penetrated into the very heart of each word of the Bible to reveal the light within the holy text was a joy to behold and a lifelong inspiration.

At the end of each lesson during the Sabbath, as the darkness was gathering, we sat in a circle. He sang his *niggun* songs of sadness and loneliness, of triumph and joy, lighting a fire in our souls, never to be extinguished.

Sometimes we walked with our teacher to nearby gardens, joining hands and singing along with him. The echo of these songs resonates within me even now as I write these words, and the inner vision of those moments will never fade.

Dr. Heschel always emphasized that we live in time rather than in space and what is truly precious are our moments rather than our possessions. That perspective has been interwoven into my own philosophy of life.

I also owe to Dr. Heschel a debt of gratitude for his vision of "radical amazement" that has also become part of my own perspective. Dr. Heschel speaks of "radical amazement" as a basis for experiencing God. He defines radical in its original meaning of "root." The essential "root amazement" is standing in awe and being open to the mystery, the beauty, the holiness of the world and existence.

Life and man and this world are simply amazing beyond our ability to reason or grasp, says Dr. Heschel. Take it in. Don't take anything for granted. Look at everything each moment of each day with that sense of wonder. That's the root for progress in science and research. That's also the root of religion.

Dr. Heschel revealed to us moments in his Hasidic home life where he sensed divinity and grace. I know whereof he speaks because whenever we were with him, we experienced that greater presence.

I am also aware of that greater presence in those *niggunim* that Dr. Heschel taught me. These wordless, melodious, and soulful songs are a great comfort to me in times of unusual stress and in moments of joy. At moments when something overwhelms me, they flow forth to lift me up, carry me, and soothe me. I never know when these songs will well up from the hidden, living wellsprings of my spirit. But they are always there within me, stored in a vessel containing accumulated tears of past losses as well as the tears of treasured past joys too deep for words.

Just recently those *niggunim* took me by surprise when I visited a patient in the hospital. When I entered the room, the "no food or liquid" sign alerted me that the patient was due for surgery. His wife was present. With a forced smile she was trying to be brave. Sam, the patient, was tense but reassured me that he was realistic, that he had everything under control, and was prepared for the worst.

Sam impressed me as a very capable, successful man used to being in command. He was counting on his iron will and determination to pull him through. Prayer was not his thing. His wife and friends were there to give him support.

Talking very forthrightly, Sam revealed the seriousness of his situation. He said he knew that his surgery was a desperate gamble and that the odds were against his survival. As we spoke, the attendant arrived with a stretcher to take him to the operating room. With the situation so grave and the tension so high, I took a risk and ventured, "Would you like me to say a prayer for you?"

For a moment Sam hesitated and then nodded in assent. I took hold of one of his hands and his wife held the other and I began the prayer for health and life and courage.

Tears welled up in Sam's eyes and he let go. He wept, his body shook. We held on in tears. Gradually he regained control. We remained in silence but in love. Sam then got off the bed, went into the bathroom, washed his face, took a towel, and wiped his face and eyes dry. He came back, grasped my hand, and said, "Thanks, Rabbi, I feel a lot mor hopeful." He mounted the stretcher and was wheeled away.

His wife stayed in the room. When he was out of sight, we embraced. She wept and I wept with her. When she regained composure, I felt the hidden wells of the *niggun* music gathering force. When the pressure mounted, I said, "Do you mind if I sing some *niggunim* taught to me by Dr. Heschel, my teacher, a Hasid and philosopher? This music is unique and there are very few living heirs to it."

"Yes, please," she responded. I began to sing these melodies, first softly, searching and feeling my way, then with mounting passion and power. Wordless strains of silence, of sadness, rising gradually into triumph.

I sang with all my *neshama*, my soul, and feeling poured into these *niggunim*. Holding my hand, she listened and we were both carried along by these ageless melodies. When I finished, she sat in silence for a moment. "That was wonderful," she said. "They touched the very depths of my being."

A favorite quotation of Dr. Heschel from the Psalms—"To you, O Holy One, silence is praise"—has assumed special significance to me. In these *niggunim*, the silence of finding our song and our meaning wells up from the depths of anguish and pain and the joy and grandeur of living. This is "soul music" more expressive than words.

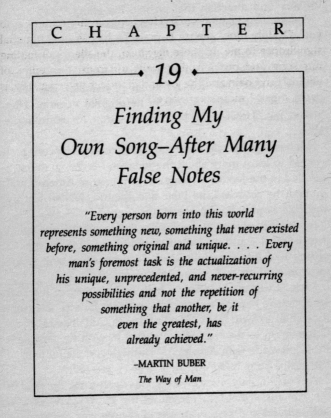

CHAPTER

• 19 •

Finding My Own Song–After Many False Notes

"Every person born into this world represents something new, something that never existed before, something original and unique. . . . Every man's foremost task is the actualization of his unique, unprecedented, and never-recurring possibilities and not the repetition of something that another, be it even the greatest, has already achieved."

–MARTIN BUBER
The Way of Man

It took me many long years before I finally found my own true song, with plenty of off-key notes along the way. However, I believe it was well worth waiting for and working toward.

I suppose I was ready to face the music from the time I decided to become a rabbi. Or did I decide? I'm still not sure exactly how it came about. As I look back, it seems that my career choice—or calling, as some say—was determined partly by studies that interested me and largely by God's guidance and direction that pushed me along.

A committed Zionist in my teenage years, I decided at age twenty to immerse myself in a total Jewish environment. That's when I left Cincinnati for Yeshiva University in New York to study the Bible and the Talmud. There I perfected my Hebrew to make the treasure house of Judaism, the Bible, and the Talmud, open to me in its original version. That thrilled me. However, I had no intention of becoming a rabbi.

Not having a specific career goal after completing college, I wanted to learn more about the Judaism I loved so much. I enrolled in the Jewish Theological Seminary of America and studied the sources—the Bible and Talmud, Jewish history and philosophy, Jewish literature.

In my third year at the seminary I took a year off and spent it in Israel. I could no longer continue my studies without setting foot into the Holy Land. That year was one of the most rewarding and memorable of my life.

I wanted to go to Israel to help build a way of life that would make real the words of the prophet Isaiah: "For from Zion shall go forth the word of the Torah, God's teaching and illumination to the world." I tied that in with the covenant that God made with Abraham: "Through you the families of the earth, your offspring, they will be blessed."

As I saw it, part of the blessing was to return to the land of our dreams and God's presence—the Holy Land—and to help rebuild and restore it. The challenge was tremendous because the land was ravaged and a good part of it was arid.

Looking back, it seems that various events, without my being aware at the time they occurred, opened doors to opportunities for challenge and growth, edging me along to where I could sing my own song and find my own meaning.

I'm referring to my traumatic accident leaving me a survivor; the loving environment of my parents who sustained me; Rabbi Feinberg, a special human being who showed me a path; Dr. Heschel, a great mind and spirit, who lit a light within me; and Israel, where I was present at a watershed of Jewish history, a miraculous moment in the two thousand years of our tragedy and grandeur—the proclamation of the establishment of the Jewish state.

Standing guard at the gates of Jerusalem, I participated in the overwhelming excitement of my people the day the United Nations took its vote. I remember journeying into the center of Jerusalem and beholding in horror the rows of bodies draped in white sheets. The remains of those young people who had died in battle had been brought to be buried in the holy soil of Jerusalem.

Not just a bystander, I experienced the thrill of working on a kibbutz, helping to rebuild the waste places of my people. I was there in the joys and the sorrows, singing Heschel's *niggunim*, my songs now, within me in my depths.

The promised land of my people, my people's history of destruction and survival, of transcending, became real to me. Israel is part of my being and my dream and my goal, for I hope someday to settle in Jerusalem and strike roots there. When my year in Israel was over, I returned to New York with exuberance and renewed zest for learning all I could about Judaism.

I completed my studies at the seminary and was ordained. Almost before I knew it, I had become a rabbi! I had no special calling, or so I thought at the time. However, I was determined to do what I could to help my compatriots discover the treasures I had found—the life of the mitzvah, of the joy of doing the good deeds commanded by a divine mandate. This way of life made me feel good and I hoped to influence others along the same lines.

I also had the feeling that the rabbinate would not necessarily be my life's work. Deeply ideological, I wanted ultimately to return to Israel and help rebuild my people's heritage and, through my people, to bring myself and others closer to God in the Holy Land.

However, there was certainly a lot for me to do at home first. I threw myself with zeal into my rabbinical duties, married, raised a family. And here I am, some thirty years later, still dreaming of Jerusalem. At the same time, I admit I am in love with New York and the excitement of its creativity and openness, and with the glorious sweep of this beautiful and majestic country and the exhilarating ways of our democracy.

My years in the rabbinate have had their ups and downs. I did not find my own true song and my life's meaning until I had suffered losses and defeats together with occasional triumphs over a thirty-year period during which I served in half a dozen congregations in different sections of the country.

The position at Memorial Sloan-Kettering, made available for me by the New York Board of Rabbis, is one that, unwittingly, I have prepared for all my life. It encompasses my experience in pastoral and rehabilitation counseling, my doctoral work, my own experience with death and dying and saying good-bye, the pain involved, and harking back to the awareness that I am a whole person even if part of me is missing. All these gave me the strength to say to myself, "Look, you've survived and now you're really going to go ahead."

The freedom and space to grow encouraged me to find my own song, do my best work. It brought me in touch with my *neshama*, my soul, and with my own image of God within me. I was able to integrate all my experiences and religious perspective and focus my specialness full force onto my human relationships. So empowered, I can reach out to the specialness of others and encourage their growth. In return, they nourish my growth.

In Heschel's words, I experience "radical amazement," seeing everything new each day with undiminished wonder. This constantly fascinates me and gives me no rest. So much still to do, so much to reach out, to give and to take, to enjoy. My song, I feel, will never truly end.

You don't have to be a rabbi to discover your own true song. Deep inside you will know when you have it right. That's when you feel good about the path you have chosen and the things you are doing with your life. We are what we are, but we must strive to become what we are capable of becoming.

There are no hopeless situations in life; there are only people who have lost hope. Mark Twain wrote about the man who wasted many years in prison because he didn't realize that his jail door was unlocked. Many doors that we consider closed will open if we just summon the vision and the will to try them. When you unlatch the right door, your own special song will emerge loud and clear—and you'll be on your way to finding your life's meaning.

• 20 •

For Good People Everywhere Who Are Hurting

"Heaven is not to be won by rest and ease and quiet. Only those who have suffered and endured greatly have achieved greatly. . . . Man has ever risen nearer to God by the altar stairs which lead through darkness, forever upwards, toward the very Throne of God."

—ALFRED ADLER

You don't have to be a patient in a hospital to know what it's like to suffer, endure, and courageously carry on. That is the lot of good people in every walk of life. I know this well from the details of their lives that my congregants share with me. This was brought home vividly during a recent memorial service on Shevuot (Pentecost), a holiday celebrating the revelation of the Law on Mount Sinai.

The synagogue is packed. I am seated on the *bimah*, a

raised platform, waiting to begin the prayer service for the dead. And I see this person sitting there with his story writ large in his eyes. Another story is told by the furrows of a face. Others in their body language speak to me of burdens and the hurt about which I know, as their rabbi. People confide in me, sometimes even more than in their family members or their close friends.

My eye travels from congregant to congregant and the stories unfold and change. And I am filled with love, with sadness, and yet with pride. These are the people who never make the headlines. They struggle silently and carry their burdens without complaint, and hang on. These are the unsung heroes so much to be admired who keep the world from going under in spite of the politicians who make the big decisions, bringing us ever closer to the brink.

For a moment I close my eyes and my mind wanders. I recall a recent letter written in graceful flourishes. The sender's name was unknown to me. I tore open the envelope and read, "Dear Rabbi, I wanted to write this letter for a long time but held back. I am a member of your congregation, though you may not know me."

I read on. "I always find your sermons inspiring and uplifting, but your talk at the last memorial service touched me most deeply. You spoke about trials we all experience or face in life, that wealth is not measured in material possessions but in other riches if we can only perceive them. I've had a hard life but, thank God, experienced many joys as well."

She continued. "When my beloved husband died suddenly twelve years ago, I went into shock. My children gave me support in my trial. They are good children and I am truly blessed. I am now self-supporting. I travel to and from work four hours each day but that's not important. I enjoy getting out and the company of my fellow workers. And the money comes in very handy. I want to thank you for helping me focus on the good things I possess. Sincerely, Regina."

I was moved by the letter, sensing a deep loneliness. I lifted the receiver and dialed her number. Regina was surprised by my call, apparently not expecting me to respond. I told her how much I appreciated her taking the time to tell me her feelings. "That encourages me," I told her. "Your feedback tells me people are listening."

Looking around at the members of my congregation, I recognize Regina. Our eyes meet and she smiles at me. She is sitting next to her son, a serious-looking young man. I think to myself, this woman is hurting. She is living with her losses and bravely carrying on. I think about the many people who are hurting.

I recall a conversation with my friend, Rabbi Harold Kushner, who wrote *When Bad Things Happen to Good People*. I met him after he had written his best-selling book that has brought so much comfort and strength to people who have experienced losses.

Rabbi Kushner told me that in the deluge of letters from people in every level of life and in his speaking engagements and question-and-answer periods, one thing was quite evident. He was absolutely amazed by the recurrent theme that overwhelmingly appeared. "You know, Pesach," he said, "many people out there are hurting."

Waiting there on the *bimah* for my turn to lead the services, my recollections continued. I remember the anguish of a married woman in her mid-years who discovered that her devoted husband of many years was carrying on an affair with another woman. She was absolutely devastated, and she came to me in despair. "What shall I do, Rabbi?" I did my best to comfort her, but it took her a long time to regain her dignity and self-respect.

Then there was a colleague who called one day. "Pesach, I visited a patient in the hospital today. He's in deep depression and panic. He says he'll kill himself if the doctors amputate his right leg, as they say they must to save his life.

I couldn't dissuade him. Can you help? You have an amputation. Maybe he'll listen."

I rush over to the hospital to visit him. I enter the room. Here's a young man, thirty-five years of age, powerful build, 230 pounds, all muscle. He tells me he's a construction worker. It's difficult physical work requiring strong hands and legs. Without a leg he'll lose his job, be a cripple, and his life will not be worth living.

He is dumbfounded when I show him my prosthesis. It helps convince him that a productive life could still be possible even after surgery. From then on his path was upward.

I look up. There are still a few moments before I am to begin the service. Closing my eyes, I wince at the memory of the pain and panic in the eyes of the mother and father whose teenage daughter had died in an auto accident after a late-night party. They had been drinking and the car went over an embankment, killing all the occupants.

The scene at the home was heartbreaking. Relatives and friends were milling around, wailing and weeping. The mother grabbed my arm. "Rabbi," she moaned, "we made a terrible mistake. We gave her too much freedom." The father was sobbing, his body shaking. "Too late now, too late," he repeated.

Images flash through my mind of grown children who come to me, their emotions raw with concern. "Mother is too old to remain home alone," a worried daughter tells me. "She's very independent, but now she forgets, and I'm afraid she will hurt herself or wander off. The neighborhood is bad but she has lived there all her years. She knows the neighbors, they take care of her. She refuses to move. But now it's dangerous. She can't live alone, and I am torn by guilt."

My mind shifts to the time-lined face of the widower in his eighties, still vibrant and strong-willed, caring for his wife, his lifelong companion, who had a stroke and couldn't speak or move or feed herself. He remembers his loving mate, the years they struggled together in the business. She was sweet and the customers loved her.

"We worked together and made the business a success," he tells me. And now she sits helpless in her wheelchair, and he takes care of her with great tenderness and love, speaking to her, encouraged by the slightest flick of a movement of the eyelid. Maybe she hears or understands.

So many people out there are hurting, facing difficulties with so much fortitude and faith and courage. I was reminded of the story of a deeply depressed man who came to his doctor. He poured out his heart; he was desperate; he just couldn't carry on or shake off his depression. He couldn't concentrate and so his work suffered. He was miserable at home with his wife and children. After pouring out his woes, he asked the doctor for help.

"What you need," the doctor told him, "is not medication but a good laugh. Take your wife to the theater to see Carlini the comedian. He packs the house every night. His humor convulses the audience."

"But, Doctor," cried the patient, "I am Carlini!"

I came back from my reverie. There they were—the men and women of my congregation. A sea of faces looking up at me, their rabbi and spiritual leader. I know each one's story. Their joys and hidden fears, their successes and disappointments, their hopes and their faith, their bravery. I was moved to compassion and tears and pride.

At last the time arrives for my Shavuot sermon. Moved by these thoughts and feelings, I chance something I'd never done before in all my years of preaching. As we begin the *Yizkor* (memorial service) for the deceased mother, father, child, friend, I ask my congregants if they would follow me and close their eyes.

I say, "We have come from the world of secular time which pressures us to accomplish and to perform and we're always rushed, to that different world of eternal time, of memories which now surround us.

"As you are seated here, close your eyes and be there in the room or wherever you choose with your loved one who has died. Bring him or her to life again in your mind, in your memory. Be there with them. See your mother or father or child or friend, whomever you choose, and recall a happy moment or moments. Now take a deep breath."

I breathe deeply. "Relax, close your eyes, and recall your loved ones now to memory." I close my eyes too. A palpable silence fills the sanctuary like a soft, loving caress. One minute, two minutes pass. We breathe deeply. We are into our memories.

"Now open your eyes," I gently tell them. I open my eyes and look out over the sea of faces, and I am surprised. Their eyes remain shut, as if they want to hold on, to play out those memories. I wait until they are all there again with me. It is a powerful, moving moment. They have preached their own sermon. It has floated upon the living stream of life so many good memories that it evokes warmth and love, so many painful memories that it fills eyes with tears and grieving, the pain and wrench of letting go. And I know that that is life, gains and losses, and there is no way to escape it.

In this chapter I have written about the members of my congregation, but my message is universal. Sooner or later, good people everywhere must face the anguish of parting from a loved one. There are no exceptions. As the ancient Yiddish proverb holds, "Not to have had pain is not to have been human."

Astronomers can foresee where every planet in the sky will be at any specific moment in the future, but our human affairs are not predictable. We can never be sure what any day holds for us. However, there is one thing we do know— we have choices. When sorrow strikes, we have the choice of becoming bitter or better.

It is up to each of us individually. We can bemoan our fate and become diminished as people or use the time of trouble to grow in compassion and appreciation for all that life has to offer. We have the capacity, as the Psalmist wrote, to "pass through the valley of tears and convert it into a life-giving fountain." And the choice we make can either impoverish our souls or nourish them.

• 21 •

The Most Important Drive of All—the Drive for Meaning

"When any human being, however obscure, decides to follow the more benevolent of the courses presented before him, the dynamic good in his choice explodes and penetrates through all the communities of man."

–EDMOND CAHN
The Moral Decision

There are many bad things that happen to us because of circumstances beyond our control. Some call such unhappy events the work of luck or chance. My own belief is that life and its happenings are a mystery. Who can explain birth and death? Our perspectives are too limited.

The loss of my leg was a terrible blow to my parents but to me it has turned out to be a bittersweet gift. I do not justify or understand why it happened, nor would I choose it. But I do know that it changed my life, making me more sensitive, more understanding, and hastening my growth. I saw that God created us out of clay and every piece of clay has a crack in it. I learned that I could be whole even though part of me is missing.

As Ernest Hemingway put it: "The world breaks everyone, and afterward many are strong in the broken places." However painful the accident was to me, it helped me find my song. The fact that I might have died under the streetcar wheels makes each day more precious. With the awareness that my life is a gift comes gratitude. I am filled with appreciation for my blessings.

Sometimes, when a patient or a member of my congregation is depressed and feels overwhelmed by his circumstances, I utilize a little exercise to help him focus on the brighter side. I place a dot in the middle of a page of white paper, thus:

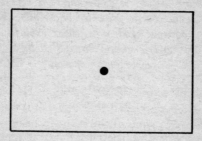

Then I ask, "What do you see?" Perhaps your response is similar to the one I invariably get. Virtually every respondent tells me he sees a black dot. "But there is more than that present," I tell them. "Most of the page is filled with whiteness, and that is overlooked."

"Isn't that the way it is with life?" I point out. "When bad things happen to us, that dot blocks out everything else. Just place your hand in front of your eyes and you can block out the tallest skyscraper, the entire world."

When we suffer any serious loss or disappointment or the inevitable separation from a loved one, we are prone to ask, "Why me?" But how many of us appreciate the large white area on the page which represents the goodness and blessings that also fill our space? How many ask, "Why me?" when all the good things are happening to us? Appreciating our blessings while we have them makes all the difference between living a fulfilling life or a life of failure and frustration.

This realization was brought into sharper focus for me recently during a group meeting in which I participated with a group of Protestant chaplains. After discussing what common religious resource we could use to help a patient, we chose the Twenty-third Psalm.

The person who wrote that psalm that brings so much strength and trust and faith to people didn't have it easy. He surely was a good man, a sensitive soul, a person of faith, and here he was in terrible pain and fear, facing death. "Though I walk through the valley of the shadow of death . . ." What gave him the courage to continue through the darkness in this strange, terrifying place until he reached the end of the valley and emerged into the light?

The chaplains pointed to trust in God. He wasn't alone, isolated, abandoned. He felt God was there, walking beside him, as if he were lying down in green pastures. The still waters—a sense of calm. Here was God's support. "Thy rod and staff, they comfort me." He then takes a leap of faith. In the English texts it says, "Surely goodness and mercy shall follow me all the days of my life."

As we read the psalm together, I tracked the wording in Hebrew, its original language. "Wait a minute," I told them. "It doesn't say *follow me* in the Hebrew. That's a wrong translation. The Hebrew wording means *pursue me*, thus, 'Goodness and mercy shall *pursue me* all the days of my life.'"

We agreed that a different perspective can flow from that simple change in wording. If goodness and mercy are pursuing us, it means that we spend a good part of our lives running. As a result, goodness and mercy have fallen behind and are never going to catch up unless we realize that life's greatest treasures are there for us if we just pause to appreciate them.

This is part of an approach I use with a patient when he feels that everything is out of control, that he is worthless and is consumed with guilt because he has become a burden. I try to help him regain his dignity and his sense of freedom to act by asking him to tell me stories from his life.

I ask the patient what made him feel good and to give me actual illustrations, especially of the times he overcame difficulties, large and small. I'm looking also for remembrances of worthwhile special things that he did, not necessarily related to success in business or a profession. Even if he says he just took care of a mother or a father or a child, it helps to restore his self-esteem. Everyone has done things of which he is proud. Recalling these events helps a person shore up his waning feelings of dignity.

Looking back at our accomplishments can be very rewarding and put aging in proper perspective. Viktor Frankl, writing about his life, said, "I don't think I want to be young again. Look at all the trials and the tribulations, the suffering that people go through when they're young to make something of themselves."

Viktor Frankl compared the days of his life to the sheets of a calendar. Instead of ripping off each page and discarding it, Frankl removes each successive leaf from his calendar and files it carefully away after jotting down a few diary notes on the back. He can reflect with pride and joy on all the richness set down in these notes, on all the days of his life he has already lived to the full.

Frankl saw each day filled with significant experiences—

moments when he enjoyed and experienced, when he suffered and somehow was able to transcend and enter in greater depth into himself and into his experiences with people. "I look back in these calendar pages," he said, "and it's kind of the harvest of the sheaves, a golden harvest."

As Viktor Frankl came to realize, each of our days is precious and irretrievable. And every moment is a new beginning. The British novelist Margaret Storm Jameson put this truth in memorable words:

> I believe that only one person in a thousand knows the trick of really living in the present. Most of us spend fifty-nine minutes of every hour living in the past, with regret for lost joys, or shame for things badly done (both utterly useless and weakening)—or in a future we either long for or dread. Yet the past is gone beyond prayer and every minute we spend in the vain effort to anticipate the future is a moment lost. There is only one world, the world pressing against you at this minute. There is only one minute in which you are alive, this minute—here and now. The only way to live is by accepting each minute as an unrepeatable miracle. Which is exactly what it is—a miracle and unrepeatable.

That's a concept I try to convey to my hospital patients for whom the quality of life in the present is increasingly important. When I approach a patient, I see him as unique and special, a feeling reinforced by one of the central texts in Judaism. It appears in the section of the Talmud entitled "Sanhedrin," which means "courts," and describes how you set up a court and administer justice. Parts are technical but, suddenly, like a comet streaking across the dark sky and lighting it up, is an illuminating text. Paraphrased, it goes like this:

> How do you admonish witnesses who come to bring testimony against someone in a capital crime? This is what you say to them: "Perchance you heard this from someone

else. Hearsay. This is not admissible evidence. Perhaps you heard it from someone you respect very much. Not admissible. Perhaps you saw this person going into the woods and coming out with a knife dripping with blood but you hadn't seen the crime occur. Not admissible."

The text continues, quoting a section from the Book of Genesis after Cain killed Abel: "Know you," God said, "the voice of your brother's bloods is crying out to me." In the Hebrew text it clearly states "bloods" in the plural rather than in the singular. That's because when Cain killed Abel, he also killed all the generations after him. The text goes on:

Know you then that you must be very careful in bringing evidence against this person, because if you destroy one person, it's as if you destroyed a whole world, and the other way around, if you keep alive one person, it is as if you've kept alive a whole world.

A beautiful, magnificent thought. One person is a world unto himself. The text reinforces this image by the tale of an earthly king who mints identical coins. Then it tells of the King of Kings, who mints many human beings from the original mold of Adam. Although physical appearances may be similar, each person is very different emotionally, spiritually, and in potential accomplishment. And so, the sages say, every human being can rightly believe, "For my sake the world was created. I am unique. There never was and never will be someone like me. I'm special. And when I'm removed, something irreplaceable is removed from the world. I'm in the image of God."

In other words, there is part of the divine within each of us. That's why the human being is always striving. As the flower turns toward the distant sun for nourishment, so each soul is drawn toward that oversoul of the universe, toward seeking its own meaning, toward creating its own world.

When we dip into doing good deeds, relating beyond ourselves, to others and to the world, we feel that goodness within ourselves. We feel as if we have found something of our meaning. We feel as if we have taken responsibility for shaping our lives and turning toward the source of our souls.

The good deeds we do need not be earthshaking and we need not go far from home to perform them. In his inspirational book, *Say Yes to Life*, Rabbi Sidney Greenberg eloquently describes treasured gifts that cannot be bought or sold:

> What extravagant gifts are ours to bestow! A word of praise many yearn to hear, encouragement to lighten the burden of living, an hour to listen to a loved one's heart, an act of forgiveness to repair a family breach, a thoughtful deed to brighten a dreary day—these gifts we too often withhold are so desperately needed and so amply at our disposal.
> As we bestow these gifts on others, they come back to enrich our lives.

This is the path to finding meaning in our lives. Meaning can be achieved only when we relate to another human being or to a cause greater than ourselves. Possibly the greatest illustration of this appears in the biblical account of how Moses delivered God's words to his people. It gives insight into human character and the consequences of finding—or losing—your meaning in life.

As related in the Book of Exodus, Moses ascends Mount Sinai, stays there for forty days and forty nights, receives the tablets of stone on which are engraved the Ten Commandments. Coming down, his face is streaming, light coming through, until he sees his people dancing around the golden calf. He becomes so angry at this betrayal that he dashes the stones to the earth, smashing them. Then he returns to Mount Sinai, remains another forty days and forty nights, and the second tablets are revealed to him. He descends, and his people receive God's words.

Now, that's the biblical version. However, the *Midrash*, a rabbinical commentary on the scriptures, perhaps can give great insight into what occurred. The rabbinical scholars could not accept the fact that Moses was so angry that he could break the tablets with the divine words. Moses was angry, but not that angry. According to the midrashic interpretation, when Moses saw the idolatrous worship the divine letters flew heavenward and he was left only with the stones. They became so heavy that no human being could carry them, slipped from his hands, and were shattered.

When Moses saw the betrayal of all he stood for, says the Midrash, he had lost his purpose, his goal for his people, his meaning. He was a failure. Everything became too heavy for him to bear and he dropped the stones.

The Midrash relates that when Moses came down from Mount Sinai the second time, the stones carried him, rather than the other way around. That's because when he saw that his people were accepting the divine revelation, his strength, spirit, and meaning returned.

In life, there is always the possibility of losing our way, of becoming depressed and feeling that things are out of control. There's no hope and you feel cut off from yourself and from your fellow man, from the world, and from God. At that point you cannot carry those heavy stones. Life's burdens are just too much to bear.

Just as Moses lost his meaning and became depressed, lost his strength and then regained it, so we have the resources within ourselves to transcend our losses, restore our own power and courage, find our meaning, and open ourselves to hope even when all avenues seem closed. Each of us must find our special meaning in our way.

Nowhere is this more true than in a hospital where there is catastrophic illness. It seems like an unlikely place to look for answers to life. Yet it is here, in an environment of great stress and pressure, that many patients pass through the crucible of pain and despair and find their meaning. I see it every day when I make my rounds.

"Rabbi," the patient confides, "before this illness I held a responsible and highly prestigious position in industry. Surely I was a 'success.' I had reached the top. It means nothing to me now. Nothing. I had sacrificed my wife and children to get there. I see now that I was a child; now I'm a grown man. I feel a tremendous power. I'm born anew. Nothing can frighten me, not even death. I see my priorities so clearly. Each day, life is precious.

"I want to travel, read, plant my garden. Each day I tell my wife 'I love you,' and I treasure the hours we spend with each other. I'm patient with my children, spending more time with them, giving them more love, and reaching out to friends. And when I leave the hospital, I'll be a different boss, listening and encouraging more."

Continuing with added intensity, his eyes glowing, the patient tells me: "Life has been good to me, even with its occasional disappointments. I want to repay in gratitude. I will dedicate some of my time to a worthy cause." He has found his meaning.

This same conversation is repeated time and again, in different words. The teenager, an excellent basketball player who went through a difficult bone marrow transplant and survives, tells me: "I'm wise now and more mature; I've learned a lot. I know what I want and who I am. I'm in a different world from my friends. It's a new ball game now." He says this with a confident smile as he leaves the hospital. We hug. He is on the way to finding his meaning.

I enter the room. The elderly woman smiles at me. "I've so much now to say and share with my husband, children, and grandchildren. I was closed. No more painful aloneness. Now I'm wide open, sharing my life and feelings—things I've never said before." She has found her meaning.

In the hospital, people become aware of life's eternal

values. That's why the hospital experience can serve as a kind of searchlight to illuminate the dark places of our lives, to bring them into the open, to help us live richer, more creative, more fulfilling, more meaningful lives.

How is meaning realized? According to Viktor Frankl, it is realized through the values that are lived and acted upon each moment. These are creative values of giving to the world, experiential values of taking in from and just plain appreciating the world and all its riches and wonders, and attitudinal values, the positive way we respond to life's hard knocks.

On Yom Kippur, the holiest day in the Jewish calendar, the day of atonement, services are completed with a prayer: "Open to us a gate even as the gates are closing." There is always a gate. We just have to find it and never lose heart. We need courage and the insight that life is a gift. We must be grateful for every moment and for blessings, past and present. We must also realize that losses are an integral part of life. We must use these inevitable losses creatively, like rungs on a ladder, to achieve a higher awareness of our perceptions, feelings, emotions, and our humanity. That's what the poet William Wordsworth had in mind when he wrote: "A deep distress hath humanized my soul."

Even when we try to think positively, we all have depressed days when life is hard to face. You turn over in bed when the alarm rings and have a washed-out feeling. Oh, another day. How am I going to make it? Why am I getting up in the morning? Then you read the newspaper at breakfast and the news is bleak. Killings, drugs, AIDS, nuclear fears, famine, revolution. It's fortunate you make it to the door. But hold it. Things are not that bad. Focus instead on the good things and feel them.

He who has given us gifts and blessings which we tend to overlook—of health, family, love, friendship, excitement, freedom, all the possibilities of mind and body and spirit—can be depended upon to renew that meaning and experience in the future. There is constant renewal of the good in life. This awareness I call faith. Windows of hope are always there to open and look out even when we feel boxed in. Our challenge is to become flexible enough and patient enough to let this happen.

ABOUT THE AUTHORS

In addition to his hospital chaplaincy and lecture schedule, PESACH KRAUSS leads the Jewish Center of Kings Highway in Brooklyn, New York, where he serves a congregation of three hundred families.

MORRIE GOLDFISCHER has coauthored many works of nonfiction, including *Winning on Wall Street* with Martin Zweig.

HEARTWARMING BOOKS OF FAITH AND INSPIRATION

Charles Swindoll

☐ 27112-1 **LIVING ON THE RAGGED EDGE** $4.50

☐ 27524-0 **HAND ME ANOTHER BRICK** $3.95

☐ 27334-5 **THREE STEPS FORWARD
TWO STEPS BACK** $3.95

Robert Schuller

☐ 26458-3 **THE BE (HAPPY) ATTITUDES** $4.95

☐ 26890-2 **BE HAPPY YOU ARE LOVED** $3.95

☐ 24704-2 **TOUGH-MINDED FAITH FOR
TENDER-HEARTED PEOPLE** $4.99

☐ 27332-9 **TOUGH TIMES NEVER LAST
BUT TOUGH PEOPLE DO!** $4.95

Og Mandino

☐ 27742-1 **CHRIST COMMISSION** $3.95

☐ 26084-7 **GIFT OF ACABAR** $3.95

☐ 27972-6 **THE GREATEST MIRACLE
IN THE WORLD** $4.50

☐ 27757-X **THE GREATEST SALESMAN
IN THE WORLD** $4.50

☐ 28038-4 **THE GREATEST SECRET
IN THE WORLD** $4.50

☐ 27825-8 **GREATEST SUCCESS IN THE WORLD** $3.95

☐ 28674-9 **A BETTER WAY TO LIVE** $4.50

Heartwarming Books of Faith and Inspiration

☐ 28229 TALKING TO YOUR CHILD
ABOUT GOD, David Heller $3.95

☐ 27484 LIFE AFTER LIFE, $4.95
Raymond Moody

☐ 25669 THE HIDING PLACE, $4.50
Corrie ten Boom

☐ 27375 FASCINATING WOMANHOOD, $4.95
Helen Andelin

☐ 27085 MEETING GOD AT EVERY TURN, $3.95
Catherine Marshall

☐ 27943 BIBLE AS HISTORY, Werner Keller $5.95

☐ 27417 HOW TO WIN OVER DEPRESSION, $4.50
Tim LeHaye

☐ 26249 "WITH GOD ALL THINGS ARE $3.95
POSSIBLE", Life Study Fellowship

☐ 27088 MYTHS TO LIVE BY, $4.95
Joseph Campbell

Buy them at your local bookstore or use this page to order.